OATrageous Oatmeals

{ DELICIOUS & SURPRISING
PLANT-BASED DISHES
FROM THE HUMBLE,
HEART-HEALTHY GRAIN }

Kathy Hester

BESTSELLING AUTHOR OF
THE GREAT VEGAN BEAN BOOK

PHOTOGRAPHY BY KATE LEWIS

PAGE STREET
PUBLISHING CO.

PAGE STREET
PUBLISHING CO.

First published in 2014 by
Page Street Publishing Co.
27 Congress Street, Suite 103
Salem, MA 01970
www.pagestreetpublishing.com

Distributed by Macmillan; sales in Canada by The Canadian Manda Group; distribution in Canada
by The Jaguar Book Group.

17   16   15   14   1   2   3   4   5

ISBN-13: 978-1-62414-074-7
ISBN-10: 1-62414-074-2

Library of Congress Control Number: 2014936074

Cover and book design by Page Street Publishing Co.
Photography and Food/Prop Styling © Kate Lewis

Printed and bound in China

Page Street is proud to be a member of 1% for the Planet. Members donate one percent
of their sales to one or more of the over 1,500 environmental and sustainability charities
across the globe who participate in this program.

{ This book is dedicated to my hardworking and delightful testers,
as well as my loyal readers. I appreciate all of you more and more every year. }

{ CONTENTS }

CHAPTER THREE

COOLING BREAKFAST OATS FOR SPRING AND SUMMER 63

CHAPTER FOUR

GRANOLAS AND BARS FOR BREAKFAST AND BEYOND 83

CHAPTER FIVE

SATISFYING SOUPS AND STEWS 99

CHAPTER SIX

SAVORY OATS FOR LUNCH AND DINNER 121

CHAPTER SEVEN

DELIGHTFUL DESSERTS 151

INTRODUCTION

ALL ABOUT OATS

Just the word "oatmeal" can evoke strong memories. It takes me back to a childhood bowl of apple-cinnamon instant oats. Warming and soothing, it fortified me enough to go out into the cold to school.

But oats can be so much more if you just explore and experiment a little bit. In this book, I will show you that you can make a meal out of oats any time of the day or night. You'll be amazed by oat recipes that go way beyond adding hot water to a brown packet of instant oats.

Don't get me wrong—there's nothing wrong with instant oats. I even have a recipe for making your own on page 19. I just want to open your mind to all the surprising opportunities that are waiting inside the oats in your pantry. Think outside the carton, and make your own plain or flavored nondairy milk from oats for a thick, rich and cheap alternative. You can make it in minutes with rolled oats or within a half-hour with steel-cut oats. There are warm breakfast oatmeals for the winter and oat smoothies and overnight refrigerator oatmeal that are healthy but really taste like dessert. Make sure to try my favorite Petit Portion Banana Pudding Overnight Oats on page 70!

Make your own pantry staples for last-minute meals and treats like soy-free, gluten-free and oil-free nondairy chez powder, golden gravy mix and even an instant hot chocolate. You're almost saving money as you read this introduction! There are oatmeal sausage crumbles that are no more processed than their steel-cut oat base. Soups made creamy with puréed oats, hearty stews and a tasty Indian dal and oat roti, are included so you can travel around the world with your oats in hand. With recipes ranging from Oat-chata to Oats-bury Steaks, I am positive you'll find something your whole family will love.

SPECIAL DIETS

Oats fit in well to most special diets with one caution: If you have celiac disease or another condition that requires you to eat gluten-free, always buy oats that are clearly marked "gluten-free."

GLUTEN-FREE

While oats are naturally gluten-free, they are often cross-contaminated with other grains that do contain gluten during harvesting, transportation or storage. Some mills, such as Bob's Red Mill, have a separate packaging division to ensure that there is no cross-contamination.

I have noted on recipes where you can use substitutions to make a recipe gluten-free. I do my best to point out which ingredients you need to check for gluten, but please don't limit yourself to only checking the ones noted, because brands constantly change their ingredient lists. What is gluten-free at this time may not be in a few months. That's why it's best to buy products that are clearly labeled "gluten-free."

Soy curls are a great substitute for seitan and are not only gluten-free but are minimally processed as well. They are basically cooked soybeans that are squashed and dried, producing a great product that has a texture similar to seitan when reconstituted.

While plain tempeh is naturally gluten-free, you have to watch out for mixed grain or flavored varieties that could add gluten to the mix. If you have a food allergy, you can never read labels too much!

SOY-FREE

Most of the recipes are naturally soy-free. Obviously, if you are soy-free, you won't be choosing soy milk to use as your nondairy milk of choice. Tofu, soy curls and tempeh are used sparingly in this book but are also out-of-bounds if you want to stay soy-free for health or allergy reasons.

Use seitan or chickpeas in place of tofu, soy curls or tempeh to adapt recipes to your dietary needs.

NO ADDED OIL

In *The Engine 2 Diet*, Joel Fuhrman, MD, John McDougall, MD and Caldwell Esselstyn, MD, all encourage a plant-based diet with no oil added. My recipes are already low in fat and most can be made without oil with a few simple modifications.

Please note that the words "oil-free" and "oil-free options" throughout the book refer to items with no added oil. There may still be whole food ingredients that contain fat, like nuts, tofu or avocados.

A few changes in traditional cooking make it simple to live this lifestyle. For instance, it's easy to sauté in water or broth instead of using oil, and using nonstick sauté pans is great for toasting spices with no oil. You can also cover traditional baking pans with parchment paper if you don't have nonstick ones. For any of the sweet recipes that call for olive oil or coconut oil, applesauce, pumpkin or date purée can be used instead. The end result will not be exactly the same, but it will still taste good!

For more ideas on no-oil-added modifications, I highly recommend Susan Voisin's site, Fatfree Vegan Kitchen (www.fatfreevegan.com).

SWEETENERS

Sweeteners are always a hot topic, and with new sweeteners popping up all the time, it can be confusing. This is one of the reasons why I allow using the sweetener of your choice in so many recipes. Just make sure to taste as you go along and add a little at a time. This way, depending on what you are using, you'll stop before it gets too sweet or bitter. Depending on the recipe, you may also have to add more liquid if you are using a dry sweetener, or a little less if you are using a liquid sweetener.

My favorite combination to use is mostly stevia with a little agave nectar. I find that stevia sweetens but lacks that round mouth feel of processed sugar. A touch of agave nectar seems to fix that for me. There are a ton of different brands of stevia, and some are quite bitter. I used NuStevia brand for these recipes but Monika, one of my testers, loves Pyure. The trick to using stevia is to add it in increments of $\frac{1}{8}$ of a teaspoon, tasting until it is where you want it to be. It may seem like overkill, but once a batter is bitter, there is no going back. The more you use a particular brand of stevia, the easier it will be to judge the amount you need to use.

NUTRITIONAL INFORMATION

I have provided nutritional information for most of the recipes as a guideline. If you make one of the options or, for instance, use plain nondairy milk in place of unsweetened, it will change the nutritional information. Also the nutritional information provided for homemade oat milks, creamers and other recipes that require straining out the oats will vary according to how thoroughly the oats are strained out. This depends on the strength of your blender.

There will also be discrepancies because of brands, diet choices and the use of alternative options. Please use the nutritional information as a guideline and not as an absolute. When you make oat milk and other drinks, one thing to note is the huge range of pulp you may have left over. I usually have ½ to 1 cup (120 to 240 g), while a few of my testers had almost none. This has to do with a number of factors, but blending for a long time in a high-speed blender results in less pulp to strain out. That may seem good, but it also increases the calories. In anticipation of this, I have determined the nutritional information for the beverages using all of the pulp so you are already looking at the highest counts. To get an exact count, you'd have to get a food scientist to test each batch you make.

If you have a medical condition where you need to keep track of specifics for your health, please use your normal food-tracking program, and use the brands or substitutions that you require.

TYPES OF OATS

Please note that all the oats people eat have the hull or inedible outer layer removed. All of the various oats listed below that are used whole have about the same nutritional profile, so whether you're using long-cooking groats or instant oats, you can feel good about whatever fits your life the best.

OAT GROATS

STOVE-TOP COOKING TIME: about 1 hour

Oat groats are what you get after the hull is removed and before any other kind of processing happens. These take the longest of all the oats to cook. They have a nutty taste and a texture much like barley or farro. My favorite cooking method is to use a slow cooker since they take a long time to cook on the stove. However, if you want to cook them on the stove or in the oven, you can speed up the cooking process by soaking them overnight first. Oat groats can be hard to find in a traditional grocery store, but you should be able to find them at your local co-op, health food store or order them online.

STEEL-CUT OATS

(Also known as Irish or Pinhead Oats)

STOVE-TOP COOKING TIME: 20 to 25 minutes

These are whole oat groats that have been cut into two or three tiny pieces each with a sharp steel blade. These cook faster than oat groats but take about twice the time of rolled oats.

Steel-cut oats mimic other whole grains such as Arborio rice or millet. Their chewy texture lends itself to making a great pilaf or risotto. They also make a great breakfast in the slow cooker because they take longer to cook than rolled oats. This means they can cook all night while you are asleep! Never use rolled oats in place of steel-cut oats in the slow cooker without making major cooking time and liquid changes or you will wake up to mush instead of the oatmeal you were expecting.

STONE-GROUND OATS

(Sometimes referred to as Scottish Oats, Quick-Cooking Steel-Cut Oats or Instant Irish Oats)

STOVE-TOP COOKING TIME: 10 minutes

These oats are stone-ground, which breaks them into pieces that vary in size. The larger pieces are almost the size of a small steel-cut oat piece, but the smallest is ground fairly fine like grits or coarse flour. Because it's crushed into a meal, this is what the British call oatmeal. They call rolled oats, which Americans call oatmeal, porridge. In Scottish oats, those large chewy bits blend in with the creamier small pieces to create something unique.

It is a bit confusing to have stone-ground oats labeled "steel-cut" or "Irish oats", but with the rising popularity of steel-cut oats, it's good marketing to make whole oats easier for busy people to use. Just know that while you do get some of the chewiness that somewhat mimics steel-cut oats from the larger oat bits, if the oats are ground, then they are not really steel-cut. This means they will cook faster than steel-cut oats.

These can be hard to find, but you can order them online at Bob's Red Mill.

ROLLED OATS

STOVE-TOP COOKING TIME: 10 minutes

To make rolled oats, whole oat groats are steamed, smashed flat by heavy rollers and then lightly toasted. While thick rolled oats exist, all of the recipes that call for rolled oats in this book will work just fine with regular rolled oats, which are usually cheaper.

Rolled oats cook the fastest. Processing rolled oats into even smaller pieces creates instant oatmeal. Rolled oats are super easy to find and are often on sale, so make sure to always have some in your pantry!

QUICK-COOK OR INSTANT OATS

STOVE-TOP COOKING TIME: 5 minutes

These are made using the same process as regular rolled oats, except they are either rolled thinner, steamed longer or both. Instant oats are also ground to create a super-fast cooking oat. There's nothing wrong with using these quick cooking oats. No matter how you fit oats into your diet, you'll reap the benefits.

Be sure to look at the recipe on page 19 to get started making your own instant oats at a fraction of the cost of buying it pre-made at the store!

OAT FLOUR

This is finely ground oats. You can buy it pre-ground or just whirl some up in your blender as you need it for a fresh and cheaper alternative. Whenever oat flour is called for, you can use homemade.

EAT MORE OATS AND MAKE YOUR DOCTOR HAPPY

Eating oats daily can lower bad cholesterol, help control high blood pressure and maintain your blood glucose level, all while making you feel fuller for longer. That's not too bad for one of the cheapest foods on your grocer's shelf!

The soluble fiber in oats works on your cholesterol while the insoluble fiber keeps your digestive track running smoothly. It's a pretty amazing food. Oats have manganese, phosphorus, zinc, selenium and iron, all of which help support your immune system, bones, connective tissues and red blood cell production. This makes them especially good to eat when you're sick.

If you've ever had poison ivy or chickenpox, you have probably soaked in an oatmeal bath made with colloidal oats. Colloidal may sound fancy and expensive, and if you buy the special bath soaks you'd certainly think it would cost a fortune to make. You can make your own for pennies by using a coffee or spice grinder, however. When oats are ground extremely fine, they become water-soluble and dissolve away in your bath. Check out the Soothing Lavendar Oat Bath Soak recipe on page 184!

THERE'S MORE THAN ONE WAY TO COOK YOUR OATS

Since this is a book all about oats, I thought I'd give you a primer of basic cooking methods to experiment with. I use each of these methods in the included recipes.

SLOW COOKING

This method is great for oat groats and steel-cut oats. I love waking up to a ready-to-eat breakfast, so I use this method almost every day in the winter. In a 1½ to 2-quart slow cooker, add ½ cup (80 g) of steel-cut oats and 2 cups (475 g) of liquid, then cook on low for 7 to 9 hours.

Slow cooking breaks down the oats more than any other cooking method, so don't expect the oatmeal to be chewy when cooked this way. For this reason, I rarely cook savory steel-cut oats in the slow cooker.

STOVE-TOP

With the exception of instant, all of the oat varieties can be cooked on the stove. It freezes well, too, so you can cook a week or two in advance on a weekend prep day. The ratios to make 2 to 3 servings are below. You can always double or triple to make a larger batch.

For each of the options below, bring the oats and liquid to a boil and then lower the heat to simmer for the amount of time listed.

OAT GROATS: 1½ cups (355 ml) liquid to ½ cup (80 g) oats. Cook for 60 minutes.
STEEL-CUT OATS: 1½ cups (355 ml) liquid to ½ cup (80 g) oats. Cook for 20 minutes.
STONE-GROUND OATS: 1½ cups (355 ml) liquid to ½ cup (80 g) oats. Cook for 10 minutes.
ROLLED OATS: 1 cup (235 ml) liquid to ½ cup (80 g) oats. Cook for 10 minutes.
QUICK OATS: 1 cup (235 ml) liquid to ½ cup (80 g) oats. Cook for 5 minutes.

OVEN

As with stove-top cooking, all of the oat varieties—except for instant—can be cooked in the oven. Here's the ratio to make 6 to 8 servings. You can always double or triple to make a larger batch. This method freezes well, too.

Bake at 350°F (177°C).

STEEL-CUT OATS: 4 cups (945 ml) liquid to 1½ cup (240 g) oats. Cook for 50 to 60 minutes.
ROLLED OATS: 2½ cups (590 ml) liquid to 2 cups (320 g) oats. Cook for 30 to 45 minutes.

MICROWAVE

I have to admit that I'm not in love with microwaves, but our new house has one built into the cabinets, so I do have one in the house now. If you are making your oats at work, you may have no other choice. The measurements below make 1 serving.

SCOTTISH: ¾ cup (175 ml) liquid to ¼ cup (40 g) oats. Cook on high heat for 3 minutes.
ROLLED: 1 cup (235 ml) liquid to ¼ cup (40 g) oats. Cook on high heat for 3 minutes.
QUICK OATS: 1 cup (235 ml) liquid to ½ (80 g) cup oats. Cook on high heat for 2 minutes.

Be aware that for instant oats, you just need to add hot water and let it sit for 3 minutes. This means you can heat the water any way you please!

CHAPTER ONE

DO—IT—YOURSELF HOMEMADE STAPLES

My favorite things to cook are staples from scratch. By staples, I mean things that might normally be bought at the store, like nondairy substitutes, wheat gluten or vegan sausage crumbles. It's so much cheaper to make these staples at home, so you can rest assured that there are no unwanted additives. I learned a lot from making these recipes. I always knew oats were versatile, but even I was surprised at just how far oats can go.

With the homemade oat milk from this chapter, you can make a thick and delicious homemade yogurt or even a cashew oat cream cheese to spread on your bagel.

I'll introduce you to delicious whole food powders that can be turned into oat chez sauce, a golden gravy and even your own flavored instant oatmeal.

Steel-cut oats turn into inexpensive taco mince, sausage crumbles and pepperoni crumbles to rival anything store-bought at a fraction of the cost. The crumbles are also great sprinkled on oat biscuits with gravy on top.

MAKE-YOUR-OWN INSTANT OATMEAL

GLUTEN-FREE, SOY-FREE, OIL-FREE

Instant oatmeal was a great thing when I was growing up. I still keep some at my office and always travel with a few packets because they are lifesavers. Remember that you can alter this recipe to fit in your diet by using the sweetener of your choice.

MAKES 12 SERVINGS

3 cups (276 g) rolled oats, divided

¼ cup (55 g) coconut sugar or brown sugar

½ teaspoon stevia

½ teaspoon salt, optional

Put 1½ cups (240 g) of the oats in a blender or food processor and process until it is a mix of pieces and powder. Pour into a bowl with the other 1½ cups (240 g) of rolled oats, sugar, stevia and salt.

Mix well.

Now you have plain instant oatmeal! You can store it in a large jar with an airtight lid or put ¼ cup (40 g) each in snack-sized resealable bag. On the bags, you may want to write additional instructions:

Add ½ cup (120 ml) hot water, stir and let sit for 3 minutes.

PER SERVING: Calories 92.3, protein 2.5 g, total fat 1.5 g, carbohydrates 19.6 g, sodium 4.8 mg, fiber 2.0 g

Plain oatmeal is a little boring all by itself, so here are three ways to dress yours up. Make one batch of Make Your Own Instant Oatmeal and put into packets according to the directions. Then add one of the following into each packet. You can even make your own variety pack. Here's to no more boring oatmeal!

OLD-FASHIONED BROWN SUGAR CINNAMON: 1 teaspoon packed brown sugar and ¼ teaspoon cinnamon.

CHOCOLATE HAZELNUT: 1 teaspoon cocoa powder and 1 tablespoon (15 g) minced hazelnuts.

OATMEAL COOKIE DOUGH: 1 tablespoon (15 g) minced walnuts, 1 tablespoon (15 g) currants or raisins, ¼ teaspoon cinnamon and the smallest pinch of cloves.

EASY OAT MILK YOGURT

GLUTEN-FREE, OIL-FREE, SOY-FREE OPTION*

If you are tired of waiting for a yogurt to come in your favorite flavor, why not try to make some yourself? It's so much cheaper to make your own, even if you have to buy a container of nondairy yogurt to get yourself started. Oat milk makes wonderful yogurt, partly because of its protein content. Homemade oat milk is strained and thickens when warmed up, so it's not necessary to use an additional thickener. The consistency is closer to a pudding or Greek yogurt than a regular yogurt.

MAKES 4 CUPS (34 OUNCES)

4 cups (946 ml) water

1 cup (92 g) rolled oats or steel-cut oats

3 tablespoons (45 g) room temperature plain nondairy yogurt (*use coconut yogurt)

UTENSILS

candy thermometer

mesh strainer

funnel

Add the water and oats to a blender and let soak for 15 minutes. Blend on high until the mixture is as smooth as possible. Strain the mixture into a mixing bowl with a spout using a fine mesh strainer. Strain the mixture back into the blender and then one more time into a 4-quart Dutch oven.

Heat the oat milk to 180°F (82°C) over medium heat, but do not bring it to a boil. This will kill any bacteria that we don't want to culture. Whisk often, because the oat milk will gel some at the bottom of the pot.

Once the milk is 180°F (82°C), remove it from the heat and then let it cool to 115°F (46°C). Anything hotter will kill the cultures we will add and anything cooler than 110°F (43°C) may not cultivate the cultures. Because the milk can still lump up as it cools, be sure to whisk it every 10 to 15 minutes to keep the texture even.

Once the milk is at 115°F (46°C), mix 1 cup (235 ml) of the warm milk with the plain nondairy yogurt in a small bowl. Once combined, whisk it into the pot with the rest of the milk.

If you have a yogurt maker, follow its instructions from here. If you don't have a yogurt maker, just put the cover on the pot and wrap the pot with two bulky towels to help keep the heat in.

You can either put this wrapped pot in the oven with the light on or do what I do and put it in a microwave. In both cases, you don't need to turn on the heat. You're just using the appliance for insulation.

Let the yogurt sit untouched for 8 to 12 hours. The longer you leave it, the tangier it will get.

Once it's ready, you can leave it plain or add sweeteners, fruit or extracts to flavor it. Store it in the refrigerator, but remember to save a few tablespoons to start your next batch of homemade yogurt.

PER 1 CUP (160 G) SERVING: Calories 83.4, protein 2.5 g, total fat 1.6 g, carbohydrates 14.9 g, sodium 0 mg, fiber 2.1 g

{ 1 cup (160 g) of oats produces a very thick, almost pudding-like texture. If you prefer yours thin, you can lower the amount to ½ cup (80 g). }

CREAMY CASHEW–OAT CREAM CHEESE

GLUTEN-FREE, SOY-FREE, OIL-FREE

The cashew cream gives the oat cream a little more substance, and when cooked for a short time, the mixture gets thick. While oats have a lot of body, this cream cheese gets the weight and texture of real cream cheese from the cashews. Ruth, one of my awesome testers, told me this is an advanced recipe because it thickens so quickly on the stove. Make sure to watch it carefully when it cooks!

MAKES BETWEEN 1 TO 1½ CUPS (8.5 TO 13 OUNCES)

1 cup (237 ml) water
½ cup (40 g) steel-cut oats
½ cup (64 g) cashews
2 tablespoons (30 ml) lemon juice
salt, to taste

Put the water and oats in your blender and soak for 30 minutes.

Add the cashews to a small saucepan and cover with water. Bring to a boil, and then simmer for 25 minutes or until soft. (Alternatively, you can soak the cashews overnight.)

Without draining the oats, blend until you have a mixture that is mostly liquid. Strain it into a bowl with a pour spout, then strain it back into the blender. Add soaked cashews and lemon juice, then blend well until the mixture becomes a thick cream. Add salt to taste.

Pour the mixture into a pan and cook over medium heat while whisking until the oats start to firm up. This will happen in about 1 minute if you are using a gas stove or about 3 to 4 minutes on an electric one. It will happen fast, and if you don't whisk you will have solids at the bottom of the pan that will turn into unpleasant lumps.

Remove the cream cheese from the heat as soon as it begins to thicken. Store in the fridge in a reusable container.

You can eat the cream cheese as is or throw in a few flavor twists, as follows.

You will use half of the plain cream cheese yielded in the above recipe and mix the following in:

CHIVE AND HERB: An extra tablespoon (15 ml) of lemon juice, 1 tablespoon (15 g) of minced chives and 1 tablespoon (15 g) of a minced fresh herb of choice (thyme, parsley, rosemary or oregano).

AGAVE NECTAR AND WALNUT: ½ cup (58 g) walnut pieces and 2 to 3 tablespoons (30 to 45 ml) agave nectar.

PER 1 TABLESPOON (15 G) SERVING: Calories 43.3, protein 1.6 g, total fat 2.1 g, carbohydrates 4.8 g, sodium 0.6 mg, fiber 0.8 g

{ Make a sour cream substitute by adding ½ to 1 teaspoon salt and juice from ½ a lemon to the above recipe. The cashews in the sour cream will add a creamy texture to your favorite chili. }

DIY OAT CHEZ POWDER

SOY-FREE, GLUTEN-FREE, OIL-FREE

This is the vegan chez powder that you should always have on hand to make an impromptu dinner of Not-from-a-Box Mac and Chez (page 122), mix in a potato soup or just make a chez sauce to cover some steamed veggies. Best is that it's cheap and easy, plus it has no added oil. My tester Julie likes to put it on her popcorn.

MAKES ABOUT 2 CUPS (360 GRAMS)

1 cup (92 g) rolled oats

¾ cup (72 g) nutritional yeast

3 tablespoons (10 g) (packed well) chopped sun-dried tomatoes (not packed in oil, but still soft)

1 teaspoon salt

1 teaspoon smoked paprika

1 teaspoon mustard powder

½ teaspoon granulated onion (or powder)

½ teaspoon granulated garlic (or powder)

Blend all ingredients until the mixture becomes a powder. Store in an airtight container.

PER ½ CUP (80 G) SERVING: Calories 120 g, protein 7.0 g, total fat 2.6 g, carbohydrates 18.0 g, sodium 582.9 mg, fiber 4.3 g

Make an easy chez sauce by adding 1 cup (235 ml) nondairy milk to ½ cup (120 g) chez powder into a small saucepan and bring just to a boil. Turn the heat down to low and whisk. You need to keep stirring or the mixture will cook faster on the bottom and get lumpy.

DIY GOLDEN GRAVY MIX

SOY-FREE, GLUTEN-FREE, OIL-FREE

In the past, I always had a few packets of vegan gravy mix tucked away in the pantry. Cheryl, my grown-up picky eater, loves her mashed potatoes and gravy, so I want to be able to make some quickly. Once I made the DIY Oat Chez Powder on page 24, I realized I needed to make my own gravy mix, too. This also doubles as a soup bouillon powder and works well when you want to thicken a soup. Make sure to try it in the Biscuit-Topped Soy Curl Stew on page 116.

MAKES ABOUT 7 SERVINGS OF GRAVY

1 cup (92 g) rolled oats

½ cup (48 g) nutritional yeast

1 tablespoon (2.4 g) thyme

1 tablespoon (5.4 g) marjoram or oregano

2 teaspoons (13 g) salt, optional

1 teaspoon coriander

1 teaspoon granulated garlic or powder

1 teaspoon granulated onion or powder

¼ teaspoon black pepper

¼ teaspoon turmeric

Blend all ingredients into a smooth powder. Feel free to leave out the salt if you are on a salt-restricted diet. Store in an airtight container.

PER ¼ CUP (40 G) (ENOUGH TO MAKE ONE SERVING OF GRAVY): Calories 57.1, protein 3.1 g, total fat 1.0 g, carbohydrates 9.1 g, sodium 640 mg, fiber 2.0 g

{ To make gravy: Boil 1½ (355 ml) cups of water in a medium skillet. Whisk in ¼ cup (40 g) of DIY Golden Gravy Mix and turn the heat to medium. Whisk and let the mixture cook for 5 to 10 minutes until it thickens up. Serve over mashed potatoes, vegan chick'n patties or wherever you think a little gravy would brighten things up. }

STEEL-CUT OAT SAUSAGE CRUMBLES

GLUTEN-FREE, SOY-FREE, OIL-FREE

This is one of my favorite staples, and I keep some in the freezer all the time for last minute pizzas. The spices give it a traditional Italian sausage flavor, while the oats give it a chewy texture and the spices create the sausage color. It's at home on a pizza or sprinkled over biscuits and gravy.

MAKES ABOUT 2 TO 3 CUPS (322 TO 483 GRAMS)

1 cup (237 ml) water

½ cup (40 g) steel-cut oats

2 teaspoons (2 g) rubbed sage

2 teaspoons (1 g) marjoram

1½ teaspoons (5 g) granulated garlic

1 teaspoon basil

1 teaspoon fennel seeds

1 teaspoon thyme

1 teaspoon oregano

¼ to ½ teaspoon salt, or more, to taste

¼ teaspoon cayenne, or to taste

¼ to ⅛ teaspoon black pepper

¼ teaspoon ground rosemary or ½ teaspoon regular

Preheat oven to 350°F (177°C) and cover a baking sheet with parchment paper.

In a saucepan, add the water and oats, bringing the mixture to a boil before lowering the heat. Cook covered for 10 minutes. Mix all the other ingredients in a bowl and set aside.

Uncover the oats and cook for an additional 5 minutes while stirring to release some of the moisture. Remove the oats from the heat and add in the spice mixture, mixing well.

Spoon the oat mixture onto the parchment paper and try to distribute it as evenly as possible. Use a second piece of parchment paper to cover the mixture, flattening it as much as possible.

Bake for 10 minutes, and then remove the pan from the oven. Cut lines into the sausage with a spatula. You aren't trying to move it; this just makes more room for the steam to escape.

Bake for 5 more minutes. Then scrape and break the sausage into pieces.

Bake for 5 more minutes until it is easily crumbled. Use as a pizza topping or freeze for another time!

PER ¼ CUP (40 G) SERVING: Calories 42.5, protein 1.8 g, total fat 0.8 g, carbohydrates 7.3 g, sodium 145.3 mg, fiber 1.3 g

Try this on top of the Apple Thyme Savory Steel-Cut Oats on page 137.

PEPPERONI CRUMBLES

GLUTEN-FREE, SOY-FREE, OIL-FREE

I love the spices in pepperoni, so as soon as I made the sausage crumbles I started a batch of these. These are good sprinkled on pizza and on pasta dishes, too!

MAKES ABOUT 1 TO 1½ CUPS (161 TO 241 GRAMS)

1 cup (237 ml) water

½ cup (20 g) steel-cut oats

3 teaspoons (7 g) smoked paprika

2 teaspoons (6 g) granulated garlic

1 teaspoon basil

½ teaspoon fennel seeds

½ teaspoon salt

¼ to ½ teaspoon black pepper, to taste

¼ to ½ teaspoon red pepper flakes, optional

Preheat oven to 350°F (177°C) and cover a baking sheet with parchment paper.

In a saucepan, bring the water and oats to a boil, and then turn the heat to low. Cook covered for 10 minutes. Mix all the other ingredients in a bowl and set aside.

Cook the oats uncovered for 5 minutes while stirring to release some of the moisture. Remove from heat and add in the spice mixture. Mix well.

Spoon the oat mixture onto the parchment paper and try to distribute it as evenly as possible. Use a second piece of parchment paper to cover the mixture, flattening it as much as possible.

Bake for 10 minutes, then remove the pan from the oven. Cut lines into the pepperoni with a spatula. You aren't trying to move it; this just makes more room for the steam to escape.

Bake for 5 more minutes. Then scrape and break up the pepperoni pieces with the spatula.

Bake for 5 more minutes or until easily crumbled. Use as a pizza topping or freeze the leftovers for another time!

PER ¼ CUP (40 G) SERVING: Calories 42.5, protein 1.8 g, total fat 0.8 g, carbohydrates 7.3 g, sodium 145.3 mg, fiber 1.3 g

SOUTHERN-STYLE OAT BISCUITS

Biscuits are a huge part of Southern culture. We eat them stuffed with veggie sausage for breakfast, on the side of scrambled tofu and even under fresh summer strawberries and whipped coconut cream for dessert. This recipe adds oats to the mix. Make sure to try it on the Biscuit-Topped Soy Curl Stew (page 116) or topped with some Steel-Cut Oat Sausage Crumbles (page 26).

MAKES 8 BISCUITS

1 cup (240 ml) soy milk (*use a different nondairy milk)

1 teaspoon apple cider vinegar

1¼ cup (165 ml) whole wheat pastry flour (**use gluten-free baking mix)

⅔ cup (60 g) oat flour or rolled oats processed into a powder

⅓ cup (31 g) rolled oats

1 tablespoon (15 g) baking powder

½ teaspoon salt

¼ cup (52 g) coconut oil, chilled

Preheat the oven to 400°F (204°C). Oil a large baking sheet. Whisk the soy milk and vinegar and set aside. It will curdle and thicken slightly, creating a vegan buttermilk.

Add the whole wheat pastry flour, oat flour, rolled oats, baking powder and salt into a medium-sized mixing bowl. Cut in the coconut oil with a pastry cutter or two knives.

Mix the soy milk and vinegar mixture into the flour mixture. Sprinkle extra oat or whole wheat flour on your cutting board. Scrape the biscuit dough onto it and knead the dough until it comes together, adding flour from around the well if the mixture is too sticky to pat out. Try not to over-handle the dough.

Pat the dough out ½-inch (1.3-cm) thick. Using a cookie cutter or a wide-rimmed glass, cut out the biscuits and arrange on a prepared baking sheet. Repeat with any remaining dough until all of it is used.

Bake the biscuits until the bottoms are medium brown, about 12 minutes.

PER BISCUIT: Calories 182, protein 4.0 g, total fat 8.6 g, carbohydrates 23.3 g, sodium 340.7 mg, fiber 3.7 g

You can use a milk other than soy milk, but it won't curdle when you add the apple cider vinegar. The biscuits still come out tasty, just a tad less moist.

EASY OAT ROTI

SOY-FREE, OIL-FREE, GLUTEN-FREE OPTION*

I love Indian food. The best part is soaking up the spicy sauce with a piece of homemade Indian bread. These thin whole-grain flatbreads are easy to make and are similar to whole wheat tortillas. They're also awesome with the Indian-Spiced Tomato Soup on page 107.

MAKES 6 ROTIS

1 cup (120 g) whole wheat flour (*use a gluten-free baking blend)

¾ cup (80 g) oat flour (or 1 cup [92 g] rolled oats blended into a flour)

1 teaspoon ground cumin

1 teaspoon ground coriander

¼ teaspoon salt

1 cup (237 ml) water

Mix the whole wheat flour, oat flour, cumin, coriander and salt in a bowl. Add in the water, mixing with a spoon, and then mix with your hands until you've formed a ball of dough. Let the dough rest for 10 minutes.

Slice the dough into 6 equal pieces and roll each out into a circle on a floured cutting board. You want them no thinner than $\frac{1}{16}$ of an inch. If they are thinner than that, they will be too crispy and won't get little puffy spots on them. That's my favorite part!

Heat a nonstick pan over medium heat. Once it is hot, add a roti and cook for 15 to 20 seconds or until you see a few spots puffing up. Flip the roti with a spatula and cook on the other side for another 15 to 20 seconds.

PER ROTI: Calories 121, protein 4.4 g, total fat 1.3 g, carbohydrates 24.0 g, sodium 0 mg, fiber 3.8 g

FAT-FREE DATE CARAMEL SAUCE WITH NO ADDED SUGAR

SOY-FREE, OIL-FREE, GLUTEN-FREE

This recipe was created to go on the Caramel Delight Oatmeal on page 55, but it is also perfect for a caramel coffee or as a topping for some vegan ice cream. Best of all, this guilt-free decadent caramel sauce has no added sugar and is oil-free, too!

MAKES 1½ CUPS (355 ML)

15 pitted dates, chopped

1 cup (240 ml) unsweetened nondairy milk

1 teaspoon vanilla

pinch salt, optional

If you have a powerful blender, such as a VitaMix, take all the ingredients and purée until smooth. If you have a blender that is not so powerful, then cook all the ingredients for 15 minutes over medium-low heat. This should soften the dates enough for your blender to purée the mixture until it's smooth.

PER TABLESPOON: Calories 27, protein 0.25 g, total fat 0.2 g, carbohydrates 6 g, sodium 11 mg, fiber 0.75 g

GUILT–FREE STEVIA CHOCOLATE SYRUP

SOY-FREE, OIL-FREE, GLUTEN-FREE

Eating healthier doesn't mean you can't have a guilt-free mocha or something chocolate to dip your strawberries into. You can customize this chocolate syrup to your preferred sweetness and thickness. You can even add a little liquor to dress it up for a party or a dessert coffee! This recipe was created to go on the Caramel Delight Oatmeal on page 55.

MAKES 1 CUP (237 ML)

½ cup (40 g) cocoa

½ cup (240 ml) water

½ to 1 teaspoon stevia (I used NuStevia powder)

1 tablespoon (15 ml) agave nectar, optional

2 teaspoons (10 ml) vanilla extract

Mix the cocoa and water in a saucepan over medium-low heat. Whisk in the stevia and the optional agave nectar.

Cook until you have the consistency that you want, whisking the whole time. It can be anywhere between a thin syrup to a thick fudge.

Store the syrup in your fridge. If it thickens too much, just add a teaspoon or 2 (5-10 ml) of water and mix in. It will seem like the sauce is breaking at first, but it will come together with a few stirs.

PER 2 TABLESPOON (30 ML) SERVING: Calories 21.3, protein 1.1 g, total fat 0.7 g, carbohydrates 5.2 g, sodium 1.1 mg, fiber 1.9 g

CHAPTER TWO

WARMING OATS FOR FALL AND WINTER

I'm drawing a line in the sand between cold weather and warm weather oats. Of course, there are a few that could go either way. I don't know about you, but I eat pancakes and waffles all year long. There's no reason why you can't cross that line whenever the mood takes you.

The Gluten-Free Blueberry Lemon Waffles are a special treat in cold weather and one of my favorites. Baked Apple-Blueberry Pancake, is my vegan version of a Dutch Baby. All of this made possible through the magic of frozen blueberries! Of course, you can always use fresh ones when they are in season.

But don't fret—I have also included plenty hot steel-cut oatmeal recipes, which are what I've become known for at my blog, HealthySlowCooking.com. Most of these oatmeals are super healthy and share the same decadent flavors as some of my favorite desserts. For instance, the Caramel Delight Oatmeal is reminiscent of a Girl Scout Cookie and is made with guilt-free date caramel and stevia chocolate sauce. Hummingbird Cake Oatmeal is inspired by a Southern favorite. You can make most of these in a small slow cooker, but if you don't have one, stove-top directions have been provided.

Some people like a pinch or two of salt in their sweet oatmeals. Feel free to add some if you'd like! Now make your doctor happy and eat oats every day!

BANANA OATMEAL COOKIE PANCAKES

SOY-FREE, OIL-FREE, GLUTEN-FREE OPTION *

These pancakes are full of bananas, oats and cinnamon, plus your choice of extras, which get lightly toasted underneath as the pancakes cook. No more pre-toasting nuts for pancakes! I highly recommend adding pecans to these if you have some on hand.

MAKES 12 SMALL PANCAKES OR ABOUT 24 SILVER DOLLAR PANCAKES

DRY INGREDIENTS

1 cup (92 g) rolled oats

1 cup (132 g) whole wheat pastry flour (*use gluten-free flour blend instead)

3 tablespoons (37 g) brown sugar (or sweetener of your choice, to taste)

2 teaspoons (10 g) baking powder

2 teaspoons (10 g) cinnamon

½ teaspoon allspice

¼ teaspoon baking soda

WET INGREDIENTS

2 tablespoons (14 g) ground flaxseeds

4 tablespoons (59 g) warm water

2 ripe bananas

1 cup (237 ml) nondairy milk

1 teaspoon vanilla

EXTRAS

chopped pecans (or your favorite nut)

golden raisins

chocolate chips

sliced bananas

blueberries

FOR SERVING

maple syrup

nondairy butter, optional

Mix the dry ingredients together in a medium-sized mixing bowl and set aside. Mix the ground flaxseed with the warm water in a small bowl to thicken.

In a smaller mixing bowl, mash the bananas with a fork until you get a fairly smooth consistency. Tiny pieces are just fine. Add the rest of the wet ingredients, including the flax mixture.

Start heating your skillet or pancake pan over medium-low heat. I use a nonstick pan so I don't have to use any oil when cooking the pancakes.

While the pan is heating, add the wet ingredients to the dry and mix until well combined.

Drop about 2 tablespoons (30 ml) of batter per pancake and sprinkle your choice of extras over the top of each pancake. Cook for about 2 to 3 minutes or until you see the edges get dry. Flip and cook about 1 or 2 minutes more.

Serve with maple syrup and some nondairy butter if you want.

PER 2 TABLESPOON (30 ML) SERVING (ONE SILVER DOLLAR PANCAKE): Calories 21.3, protein 1.1 g, total fat 0.7 g, carbohydrates 5.2 g, sodium 1.1 mg, fiber 1.9 g

BAKED APPLE–BLUEBERRY PANCAKES

By whirling up the batter in your blender and cutting up a little fruit, you'll have a weekend breakfast that your family will love. Vary the fruits for each season—use fresh berries in the summer and frozen berries in the winter. The silken tofu provides a light eggy texture that makes this breakfast extra special.

MAKES 4 SERVINGS

1 cup (92 g) rolled oats

¾ cup (178g) nondairy milk

2 cups (220 g) apple chunks

1 cup (148 g) blueberries, fresh or frozen

½ container (325 g) silken tofu

¼ cup (55g) coconut sugar or brown sugar

2 teaspoons (10 g) baking powder

½ teaspoon vanilla

¼ teaspoon salt or kala namak

Preheat your oven to 350°F (177°C). Either use a nonstick 12" (30.5-cm) skillet or coat a 12" (30.5-cm) cast iron pan with some spray oil.

Let the oats and milk sit in your blender. Heat the skillet over medium-high heat and sauté the apples and berries for about 8 minutes until the apples become tender. Spread the fruit so that it's evenly distributed over the bottom of the pan, and then remove from heat.

Add the tofu, sugar, baking powder, vanilla and salt to the blender and blend well. Pour the mixture over the fruit and spread out using a spatula.

Put the skillet in the oven and bake for 15 minutes, until the center is solid and the edges start to pull back from the pan.

PER SERVING: Calories 278.3, protein 8.6 g, total fat 4.9 g, carbohydrates 58.0 g, sodium 427.3 mg, fiber 5.0 g

{ This oven pancake is my vegan version of a Dutch Baby, which is made with eggs. Kala namak is a salt that has a high sulfur content, which makes it taste eggy. }

GLUTEN-FREE LEMON BLUEBERRY BELGIAN WAFFLES

GLUTEN-FREE, SOY-FREE, OIL-FREE OPTION*

I can't help but add some lemon wherever I have blueberries! If you aren't fond of the combination, use vanilla or almond extract instead. It's very important to cook these waffles at least 5 minutes, if not more. If the waffle is not ready, it will make a mess.

MAKES 4 WAFFLES

DRY INGREDIENTS

¾ cup (69 g) finely ground rolled oats or oat flour

½ cup (48 g) rolled oats

¼ cup (39.5 g) rice flour

¼ cup (37.5 g) almond flour

½ teaspoon baking powder

pinch of salt

WET INGREDIENTS

1 cup (148 g) blueberries (fresh or frozen)

¾ cup (180 g) nondairy milk

½ cup (127.5 g) applesauce

2 tablespoons (14 g) ground flax mixed with 4 tablespoons (59 g) warm water

½ teaspoon vanilla extract

½ teaspoon lemon extract (or ¼ teaspoon lemon oil)

FOR SERVING

maple syrup

nondairy butter, optional

Mix the dry ingredients together in a large bowl until well combined. In a different bowl, combine the wet ingredients and mix well. Then pour the wet into the dry and mix thoroughly.

Set the batter aside for 10 minutes to let the rolled oats soften. Please note that this batter is very thick. Preheat your waffle iron at medium-high temperature if you have that option. The waffle iron should be hot once the batter is ready.

I suggest spraying the top and bottom plates with some spray oil, but you can make it oil-free* by just relying on the nonstick coating. If you choose to use no additional oil, make sure the waffle is completely cooked. If any of the outside is not crispy, the waffle will tear, stick and generally make a mess.

Place about ⅓ cup (80 ml) of batter in the middle of the waffle iron and spread into a circle with a wooden spoon or silicone spatula. When you place the top down, the batter will spread. If your mixture gets too thick to spread, add a little nondairy milk to loosen it up.

Cook according to your waffle iron instructions, about 5 to 8 minutes. With my waffle iron, the first waffle takes 8 minutes. As you make additional waffles, the process gets a little faster until it takes 5 minutes for each waffle.

PER WAFFLE: Calories 259.2, protein 6.9 g, total fat 7.8 g, carbohydrates 42.5 g, sodium 90.4 mg, fiber 6.1 g

Don't have a waffle iron? Add ¼ to ½ cup (60 to 120 ml) of extra nondairy milk to loosen up the batter and make pancakes instead!

BAKED MEYER LEMON STEEL-CUT OATMEAL

GLUTEN-FREE, SOY-FREE, OIL-FREE

These hands-off oats cook in 1 hour in your 5-quart Dutch oven. To make cleaning up easy, mix everything together in the same pan you're cooking in. This is perfect for brunch. You can even tidy up while it's in the oven. I love the sweet tangy taste of Meyer lemons in this.

MAKES 8 SERVINGS

4 cups (946 ml) water

1½ cups (120 g) steel-cut oats

1 cup (200 g) sugar (or ½ cup [120 ml] agave nectar)

1 teaspoon vanilla extract

zest and juice of 2 Meyer lemons

pinch of salt

Preheat oven to 350°F (177°C). Mix all the ingredients in a 5-quart Dutch oven.

Cover and bake for 1 hour. Stir well before serving. The top will look watery, but once you stir it will come together and have just the right consistency. Serve topped with a pinch of zest and nondairy milk on the side.

PER SERVING: Calories 227.3, protein 5.3 g, total fat 2.3 g, carbohydrates 47.8 g, sodium 19.4 mg, fiber 3.8 g

• Make a batch on the weekend and store it in single servings in the fridge for a ready-to-eat lunch all week long!.

• Meyer lemons not in season? Use your favorite citrus fruit in their place.

CRANBERRY ORANGE BAKED OATMEAL

GLUTEN-FREE, SOY-FREE, NO ADDED OIL

This oatmeal solves the problem of making breakfast every morning, because you make 6 servings worth of oatmeal at a time. If that's more than what you need, you can freeze single servings for another time. Serve warm with nondairy milk poured over it. Cranberry and orange is one of my favorite flavor combos, but you can vary it with the fruit and extracts you have on hand.

MAKES 6 SERVINGS

DRY INGREDIENTS

2 cups (184 g) rolled oats

1 teaspoon baking powder

½ teaspoon salt

⅛ teaspoon stevia, optional

WET INGREDIENTS

1½ cups (355 ml) nondairy milk

1 cup (110 g) fresh cranberries, minced

½ cup (122 g) unsweetened applesauce

⅓ cup (80 ml) agave nectar or maple syrup

2 tablespoons (14 g) ground flaxseed mixed with 4 tablespoons (59 g) warm water

1 teaspoon orange extract

Preheat the oven to 350°F (177°C) and oil a square 9" x 9" (23 x 23-cm) baking dish. To make this oil-free, line the dish with parchment instead.

Mix the dry ingredients in a large mixing bowl. Mix the wet ingredients in a smaller bowl.

Right before baking, pour the wet ingredients into the dry ones and mix until thoroughly combined. Pour into the prepared pan and bake for 45 minutes or until the edges turn golden brown and the middle has set.

PER SERVING: Calories 196.2, protein 4.1 g, total fat 4.1 g, carbohydrates 37.0 g, sodium 280.8 mg, fiber 4.2 g

• Top with a drizzle of maple syrup or a handful of your favorite toasted nuts.

• Make sure to save any leftovers for dessert! It's amazing with a scoop of nondairy vanilla ice cream.

APPLE PEAR BAKED STEEL-CUT OATMEAL

GLUTEN-FREE, SOY-FREE, NO ADDED OIL

I love the texture of steel-cut oats, and they really shine in this baked oatmeal. Don't worry if it's a little watery on top when you take it out of the oven. Just stick a spoon in and test that it's cooked underneath. The water will be absorbed more after you remove it from the oven or can easily be mixed in when you put it in bowls.

MAKES 6 SERVINGS

4 cups (960 ml) nondairy milk

2 cups (220 g) peeled and chopped apple, about 2 medium

2 cups (322 g) peeled and chopped pear, about 2 medium

1 cup (80 g) steel-cut oats

2 teaspoons (10 ml) vanilla extract

1 teaspoon cinnamon

¼ teaspoon allspice

pinch cloves

Preheat the oven to 350°F (177°C) and prepare a large rectangular baking dish by coating it with oil or lining it with parchment.

Mix all the ingredients in a large mixing bowl.

Pour into prepared pan and bake uncovered for 60 to 75 minutes, or until the edges turn golden brown and the middle has mostly set. As the steel-cut oats sink to the bottom, the fruit will remain on top, causing the top to be more watery.

PER SERVING: Calories 215.7, protein 5.2 g, total fat 5.4 g, carbohydrates 39.5 g, sodium 10.8 mg, fiber 5.5 g

Top with a drizzle of maple syrup or a handful of your favorite toasted nuts.

PUMPKIN OAT BREAKFAST CAKE

Make this cake on a Sunday and take care of breakfast all week. It's a great way to start off pumpkin-everything season! This whole-grain cake isn't overly sweet, which allows all the spices to really shine through.

MAKES ABOUT 24 SMALL PIECES OR 12 LARGE ONES

DRY INGREDIENTS

1½ cups (198 g) whole wheat pastry flour (*use a gluten-free baking mix)

1½ cups (140 g) rolled oats

1 teaspoon baking soda

1 teaspoon cinnamon

½ teaspoon cardamom

½ teaspoon ground ginger

¼ teaspoon allspice

¼ teaspoon salt

pinch of cloves

WET INGREDIENTS

2 tablespoons (14 g) ground flaxseed mixed with 4 tablespoons (59 g) warm water

1 (15 oz) can pumpkin purée or 1½ cups (367 g) homemade

½ cup (110 g) brown sugar

¼ cup (52 g) coconut oil, melted (**use applesauce or extra pumpkin purée to make oil-free)

¼ cup (60 ml) agave nectar

Preheat oven to 350°F (177°C). Prepare a rectangular 8" x 12" (20 x 30.5-cm) baking dish by spraying with oil or by lining with parchment paper.

Mix the dry ingredients in a medium bowl and set aside. In a smaller bowl, combine the wet ingredients and mix until thoroughly combined.

Add the wet mixture to the dry mixture and mix until just combined. Pour into prepared pan and smooth the top with a spatula.

Bake for 25 to 35 minutes or until the middle starts to be firm.

PER SERVING (cut into 24 pieces): Calories 101.0, protein 1.8 g, total fat 3.0 g, carbohydrates 19.2 g, sodium 79.1 mg, fiber 2.3 g

DIANNE'S ELVIS OATMEAL

GLUTEN-FREE, SOY-FREE, OIL-FREE

If you have never heard of an Elvis sandwich, it is a peanut butter and banana grilled sandwich, sometimes with bacon. This recipe is the brainchild of my friend, Dianne Wenz, a vegan lifestyle coach. She teaches cooking classes and runs both veggiegirl.com and chicvegan.com. She uses her Elvis oatmeal recipe to keep her fueled through her busy days.

MAKES 4 SERVINGS

1 cup (96 g) rolled oats

2 cups (470 ml) unsweetened vanilla nondairy milk

2 medium bananas, sliced

½ cup (48 g) peanuts, chopped (with extra for garnish)

½ teaspoon cinnamon

3 tablespoons (48 g) peanut butter

½ cup (85 g) vegan chocolate chips

Combine the oats and milk in a large saucepan, then bring to just a boil over high heat. Turn the heat down to medium and add the banana, peanuts and cinnamon. Cook for about 5 minutes or until the oatmeal begins to thicken, then stir in the peanut butter.

Serve topped with 2 tablespoons (30 g) each of peanuts and chocolate chips.

PER SERVING: Calories 434, protein 12.4 g, total fat 24.1 g, carbohydrates 50.2 g, sodium 64.4 mg, fiber 6.8 g

{ I like to take my Elvis oatmeal to the extreme and sprinkle coconut bacon on top in addition to the peanuts and chocolate chips. But you already know I'm like that! }

PUMPKIN COFFEE CAKE OATMEAL

GLUTEN-FREE, SOY-FREE, OIL-FREE OPTION*

The best part of coffee cake is the delicious crumbly topping that gets its crunch from the nuts and some spice from the cinnamon. As you add it to your wholesome bowl of pumpkin oats, you'll swear you can see *decadence* and *healthy* holding hands!

MAKES 3 SERVINGS

½ cup (40 g) steel-cut oats

1¼ cup (437 ml) unsweetened vanilla nondairy milk (or plain plus ½ teaspoon vanilla extract)

½ cup (124 g) pumpkin purée

½ teaspoon cinnamon

COFFEE CAKE TOPPING

3 tablespoons (37 g) brown sugar (or other sweetener if you don't use refined sugar)

3 tablespoons (23 g) pecans or walnuts, chopped

½ teaspoon cinnamon

STOVE-TOP METHOD

Mix toppings together and set aside. Add the oats and nondairy milk to a small saucepan and bring to a boil over high heat. Lower to medium-low and stir in pumpkin and cinnamon, cooking for 15 to 20 minutes or until the oats are tender. Serve topped with the coffee cake topping.

SLOW COOKER METHOD

Use 1¾ cups (473 ml) unsweetened vanilla nondairy milk instead of 1¼ cups (437 ml).

The night before: Mix toppings in a small container and cover until the morning. Spray your 1½ to 2-quart crock with some oil to help with later cleanup (*or use with no oil to make oil-free and just soak with water for a few hours for easy cleanup).

Add all the ingredients except the toppings. Cook on low overnight (7 to 9 hours).

In the morning: Stir your oatmeal well. It may seem watery at the top, but stirring will create a more uniform consistency. Top with coffee cake topping.

PER SERVING: Calories 209.2, protein 5.8 g, total fat 8.4 g, carbohydrates 34.5 g, sodium 66.1 mg, fiber 5.1 g

LEMON RASPBERRY "CHEESECAKE" OATMEAL

GLUTEN-FREE, SOY-FREE, OIL-FREE OPTION*

In my original version of this, I used vegan raspberry Greek yogurt. If you can find it in your area, make sure to try it. It's a little more tart and makes the oatmeal taste a bit more like cheesecake. If you can't find vegan raspberry Greek yogurt, don't worry; it's still a huge treat with plain old vegan yogurt.

MAKES 3 SERVINGS

½ cup (40 g) steel-cut oats

1½ cups (360 ml) unsweetened nondairy milk

1 teaspoon lemon extract

½ teaspoon vanilla extract

sweetener of your choice, to taste

FOR TOPPING

1 container vegan raspberry Greek yogurt (or plain vegan yogurt with fresh raspberries)

STOVE-TOP METHOD

Add the oats and nondairy milk to a small saucepan and bring to a boil over high heat. Lower to medium-low and stir in the extracts. Cook for 15 to 20 minutes or until the oats are tender. Sweeten to taste with your favorite sweetener and serve topped with the yogurt "icing".

SLOW COOKER METHOD

Use 2 cups (473 ml) unsweetened vanilla nondairy milk instead of 1½ cups (350 ml).

The night before: Spray your 1½ to 2-quart crock with some oil to help with later cleanup (*or use with no oil to make oil-free and just soak with water for a few hours for easy cleanup).

Add everything except sweetener and yogurt. Cook on low overnight (7 to 9 hours).

In the morning: Add sweetener and stir your oatmeal well. It may seem watery at the top but if stirred it should all mix together well. Serve with the yogurt "icing" on top.

PER SERVING: Calories 185.3, protein 4.8 g, total fat 6.2 g, carbohydrates 28.9 g, sodium 9.2 mg, fiber 3.3 g

KHEER (INDIAN PUDDING) OATMEAL

Kheer is a creamy Indian rice pudding with cardamom, raisins and nuts. This oatmeal is a guilt-less and vegan version of the traditional cream-laden dessert.

MAKES 3 SERVINGS

½ cup (40 g) steel-cut oats

1½ cups (360 ml) unsweetened nondairy milk

½ teaspoon ground cardamom

¼ cup (41 g) raisins or raisin mix with berries

pinch of saffron, optional

sweetener of your choice, to taste

FOR TOPPING

chopped nuts (pistachios, cashews, almonds or assortment)

STOVE-TOP METHOD

Add the oats and nondairy milk to a small saucepan and bring to a boil over high heat. Lower to medium-low and stir in the cardamom, raisins and saffron (if using). Cook for 15 to 20 minutes or until the oats are tender. Sweeten to taste with your favorite sweetener and serve topped with mixed nuts.

SLOW COOKER METHOD

Use 2 cups (473 ml) nondairy milk instead of 1½ cups (360 ml).

The night before: Spray your crock with some oil to help with later cleanup (*or use with no oil to make oil-free and just soak with water for a few hours for easy cleanup).

Add oats, nondairy milk, raisins, cardamom and optional saffron. Cook overnight on low, for 7 to 9 hours.

In the morning: Stir your oatmeal well. It may seem watery at the top but stirring should provide a more uniform consistency. Stir in your choice of sweetener to taste and top each serving with chopped nuts.

PER SERVING: Calories 174.6, protein 5.6 g, total fat 3.8 g, carbohydrates 30.7 g, sodium 91.7 mg, fiber 4.3 g

CARAMEL DELIGHT OATMEAL

GLUTEN-FREE, SOY-FREE, OIL-FREE OPTION*

Just thinking about Girl Scout cookies makes me crave that gooey caramel coconut that's in between the chocolate stripes and the crisp vanilla cookies. I thought I'd use healthy substitutes to make a nice—even healthier—Caramel Delight oatmeal. The caramel and chocolate sauce recipes can be found in the Do It Yourself Homemade Staples chapter, which starts on page 17.

MAKES 3 SERVINGS

½ cup (40 g) steel-cut oats

1½ cups (360 ml) unsweetened nondairy milk

¼ cup (20 g) finely shredded coconut

1 teaspoon vanilla extract

TOPPING (OR MIX-INS)

2 tablespoons (30 g) shredded coconut

2 tablespoons (30 ml) Fat-Free Date Caramel Sauce with No Added Sugar (see recipe on page 32)

2 tablespoons (30 ml) Guilt-Free Stevia Chocolate Sauce (see recipe on page 33)

sweetener of your choice, to taste (you may need none since the toppings are sweet)

STOVE-TOP METHOD

Add the oats and nondairy milk to a small saucepan and bring to a boil over high heat.

Lower to medium-low and stir in the coconut and vanilla. Cook for 15 to 20 minutes or until the oats are tender. Stir in shredded coconut, caramel and chocolate sauce. Taste, adding more sweetener if necessary.

SLOW COOKER METHOD

Use 2 cups (473 ml) unsweetened vanilla nondairy milk instead of 1½ cups (360 ml).

The night before: Make the sauces (see recipes on page 32 and page 33). Spray your 1½ to 2-quart crock with some oil to help with later cleanup (*or use with no oil to make oil-free and just soak with water for a few hours for easy cleanup).

Add oats, milk and coconut and vanilla extracts. Cook on low overnight, for 7 to 9 hours.

In the morning: Stir your oatmeal well. It may seem watery at the top but stirring will provide a more uniform consistency. Either top with or stir in shredded coconut, caramel and chocolate sauce. Taste, adding more sweetener if necessary.

PER SERVING: Calories 208.9, protein 6.0 g, total fat 6.9 g, carbohydrates 30.6 g, sodium 15.4 mg, fiber 5.1 g

{ For a fancier presentation, mix the coconut and caramel together and spread stripes over the oatmeal. Then spoon the chocolate sauce in between the caramel stripes. You can also top with an extra sprinkle of coconut. }

HUMMINGBIRD CAKE OATMEAL

GLUTEN-FREE, SOY-FREE, OIL-FREE OPTION*

When nothing but something sweet will do, try some Hummingbird Cake Oatmeal. This is an old Southern cake favorite that has pineapple, banana and pecans in the cake and is topped with a vegan yogurt "icing".

MAKES 2 TO 3 SERVINGS

½ cup (40 g) steel-cut oats

1½ cups (360 ml) nondairy milk

½ cup (82 g) minced pineapple (fresh, frozen, or canned)

1 teaspoon vanilla extract

½ teaspoon cinnamon

1 ripe banana (the riper it is the less extra sweetener you'll need)

2 tablespoons (30 g) chopped pecans

"ICING"

½ cup (113 g) vanilla vegan yogurt

¼ cup (41 g) chopped pineapple

1 tablespoon (15 g) chopped pecans

STOVE-TOP METHOD

Mix topping together and set aside. Add the oats and nondairy milk to a small saucepan and bring to a boil over high heat. Lower to medium-low and stir in pineapple, vanilla and cinnamon. Cook for 15 to 20 minutes or until the oats are tender. Mash in the banana and mix in the pecans. Serve topped with the "icing".

SLOW COOKER METHOD

Use 2 cups (473ml) nondairy milk instead of 1½ cups (360 ml).

The night before: Spray your 1½ to 2-quart crock with oil to help with later cleanup (*or use with no oil to make oil-free and just soak with water for a few hours for easy cleanup).

Add oats, pineapple, cinnamon and nondairy milk. Cook on low overnight, for 7 to 9 hours. You can mix the icing ingredients in now and store in the fridge overnight. Feel free to add more sweetener if you desire.

In the morning: Stir your oatmeal well. It may seem watery at the top, but stirring will provide a more uniform consistency. In a separate bowl, mash the banana and add it and the nuts to the oatmeal. Top each serving with the icing and extra pineapple. You can add more sweetener if desired.

PER SERVING: Calories 293.1, protein 6.7 g, total fat 10.4 g, carbohydrates 43.9 g, sodium 93.8 mg, fiber 6.5 g

JENNI'S SPAR FOR THE SPURTLE, OVER-THE-TOP OATMEAL

My friend Jenni Field is the force behind PastryChefOnline.com and is the queen of cooking techniques. I knew she had a fancy oatmeal tucked away and convinced her to share it with the oatmeal-obsessed like me. The base is a rich mix of two kinds of oats topped with whipped coconut cream and maple pecans spiced with cinnamon.

MAKES 4 SERVINGS

FOR THE OATS

⅓ cup (27 g) steel-cut oats, soaked in cold water overnight

½ cup (48 g) thick cut rolled oats

¼ to ½ teaspoon kosher salt, to taste

1 tablespoon (15 ml) coconut oil

¼ cup (81 ml) maple syrup

1 cup (237 ml) water

1 cup (226 ml) full-fat coconut milk, stirred well

salt, to taste

FOR THE MAPLE COCONUT CREAM

1 can (13.5 oz [420 ml]) full-fat coconut milk, refrigerated overnight

1 to 2 tablespoons (15 to 30 ml) organic pure maple syrup, to taste

FOR THE MAPLE SPICED NUTS

1 tablespoon (14 ml) coconut oil

2 tablespoons (30 ml) organic pure maple syrup

½ cup (54 g) pecan halves and/or pieces

½ teaspoon cinnamon

Stir all ingredients for the oats together and bring up to a boil over medium-high heat, stirring frequently. Reduce the heat, cover and let simmer for 15 minutes.

Taste for texture. If the oats are a bit too chewy for your liking, put the lid back on and simmer for an additional 3 to 5 minutes.

Carefully open the can of coconut milk and spoon the thick, white part into a regular bowl, or into the bowl of your stand mixer fitted with the whisk attachment. Reserve the thin, clear portion for other use.

Either with a hand mixer with a whisk attachment or your stand mixer, whip on medium speed until it begins to loosen up a bit. Then increase to high speed. Add the salt and drizzle in the maple syrup, whipping until you have a lovely whipped consistency.

Line a cookie sheet with Silpat or parchment and set it aside, conveniently close to the stove.

In a heavy-bottomed skillet, melt the coconut oil over medium heat.

Add the syrup, nuts, cinnamon and sea salt and let sizzle, stirring constantly with a high heat-proof silicone spatula or a wooden spoon.

Test the maple syrup periodically by smearing a bit onto the Silpat or parchment. It should cool into a hard candy when it is ready. If you test it and the syrup sets up but is still gummy, keep cooking and stirring.

When the maple syrup tests done, about 5 to 7 minutes, spread the nuts out on the lined cookie sheet to cool. When cool, either leave as is or chop into pieces as coarse or fine as you like.

Split the cooked oats between two warmed bowls. Add a dollop of the maple coconut cream and a handful of the maple spiced nuts to each serving and enjoy.

PER SERVING: Calories 638.9, protein 7.7 g, total fat 45.6 g, carbohydrates 52.4 g, sodium 237.7 mg, fiber 3.9 g

PEANUT BUTTER PIE OATMEAL

This oatmeal will remind you of silky peanut butter pie, complete with a graham cracker "crust" sprinkled on top with chopped peanuts. You could get wild and throw in a few vegan chocolate chips as well.

MAKES 2 TO 3 SERVINGS

½ cup (40 g) steel-cut oats

1½ cups (360 ml) unsweetened nondairy milk

2 tablespoons (32 g) peanut butter

sweetener of choice, to taste

FOR TOPPING

crushed graham crackers and chopped peanuts

STOVE-TOP METHOD

Add the oats and nondairy milk to a small saucepan and bring to a boil over high heat. Lower to medium-low and cook for 15 to 20 minutes or until the oats are tender. Mix in peanut butter and sweetener. Top with crushed graham crackers and chopped nuts.

SLOW COOKER METHOD

Use 2 cups (473 ml) unsweetened nondairy milk instead of 1½ cups (360 ml).

The night before: Spray your 1½ to 2-quart crock with some oil to help with later clean up (*or use with no oil to make oil-free and just soak with water for a few hours for easy cleanup).

Add oats and milk. Cook on low overnight, for 7 to 9 hours.

In the morning: Stir your oatmeal well. It may seem watery at the top but stirring will provide a more uniform consistency. Mix in peanut butter and sweetener. Top with crushed graham crackers and chopped peanuts.

PER SERVING: Calories 216.7, protein 7.5 g, total fat 9.8 g, carbohydrates 25.5 g, sodium 54.2 mg, fiber 4.0 g

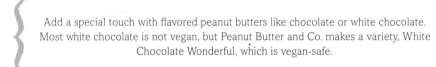

Add a special touch with flavored peanut butters like chocolate or white chocolate. Most white chocolate is not vegan, but Peanut Butter and Co. makes a variety, White Chocolate Wonderful, which is vegan-safe.

BUTTERNUT SQUASH MAPLE WALNUT SCONES

SOY-FREE, OIL-FREE OPTION*, GLUTEN-FREE OPTION**

These scones are only slightly sweet so they are just as great with a soup or salad as they are as a delicious breakfast. If you'd like them sweeter, make a glaze by adding a few drops of maple syrup to ¼ cup (60 g) powdered sugar.

MAKES 12 SCONES

DRY INGREDIENTS

1½ cups (198 g) whole wheat pastry flour (**use a gluten-free baking mix)

¾ cup (72 g) rolled oats

¼ cup (60 g) coconut sugar or brown sugar

1 tablespoon (15 g) baking powder

1 teaspoon cinnamon

¼ teaspoon nutmeg

½ teaspoon salt

WET INGREDIENTS

½ cup (123 g) butternut squash purée (see note)

2 tablespoons (14 g) ground flax-seed mixed with 4 tablespoons (60 ml) warm water

¼ cup (60 ml) nondairy milk

¼ cup (60 ml) maple syrup

1 teaspoon maple extract

½ cup (55 g) chopped walnuts

Preheat the oven to 350°F (176°C) and oil a large cookie sheet (*or line with parchment to make oil-free).

Mix the dry ingredients in a large mixing bowl. Mix the wet ingredients in a smaller bowl.

Right before baking, add the wet ingredients into the dry ones and mix until thoroughly combined, then mix in the walnuts.

Scoop out the batter to the middle of your prepared cookie sheet and pat it into a big circle about ¾-inch thick. Using a chef's knife, score into 12 triangles by cutting halfway through the dough.

Bake for 25 to 30 minutes until golden brown.

PER SCONE: Calories 100.8, protein 2.9 g, total fat 2.8 g, carbohydrates 16.5 g, sodium 200 mg, fiber 3.0 g

{ You can use canned pumpkin in place of the butternut squash if that's what you have on hand. }

CHAPTER THREE

COOLING BREAKFAST OATS FOR SPRING AND SUMMER

Oatmeal has burst out of its role as a warm-you-up breakfast to cool you down in the summer too. You can find plenty of warming breakfasts on page 35.

Refrigerator oatmeal may not sound very sexy, but once you try it, you'll find yourself wanting it every morning. Imagine waking up to banana pudding and coconut cream for breakfast. The best part is that you just need to reach in your fridge, and it's ready to go with you wherever you are headed.

Smoothies are another surprising place to tuck away your morning oatmeal. Flavors like pomegranate rose and carrot cake are a treat anytime of the day—especially for breakfast.

CANDY BAR OVERNIGHT REFRIGERATOR OATMEAL

GLUTEN-FREE, SOY-FREE, OIL-FREE

Eating these no-cook overnight oats is like eating a bowl of your favorite candy bar. Full of cocoa, coconut and almonds all mixed in with the goodness of oats and chia seeds—breakfast has never tasted sweeter!

MAKES 1 SERVING

⅓ cup (31 g) rolled oats

1 tablespoon (10 g) chia seeds

2 teaspoons (10 g) cocoa powder

1 (6 oz [170 g]) container of vanilla flavored vegan yogurt, or ¾ cup (170 ml) plain vegan yogurt and ¼ teaspoon vanilla extract

⅓ cup (79 ml) coconut flavored almond milk, or plain plant-based milk and ¼ teaspoon vanilla or coconut extract

2 tablespoons (12 g) shredded coconut

sweetener to taste, optional

Layer all the ingredients in a quart mason jar or a dish with a cover. Mix well and let sit in the fridge overnight. Stir and eat.

PER RECIPE: Calories 397.9, protein 9 g, total fat 21.9 g, carbohydrates 53.1 g, sodium 76.6 mg, fiber 11.6 g

PROTEIN PACKED PEANUT BUTTER CUP OVERNIGHT OATS (PETITE PORTION)

GLUTEN-FREE, SOY-FREE, OIL-FREE

This may be a smaller portion, but it will keep you feeling full for a long time thanks to the chocolate-flavored protein powder and powdered peanut butter. You can use fresh nut butter instead if that's what you have on hand. You can also use plain cocoa powder if you don't have any protein powder.

MAKES 1 SERVING

¼ cup (20 g) oats

1 tablespoon (16 g) chocolate vegan protein powder (I use rice-based)

1 tablespoon (6 g) powdered peanut butter (plain or chocolate) or fresh nut butter

¼ teaspoon vanilla

½ cup (118 ml) plant-based milk (plain or vanilla)

sweetener of choice, to taste if needed

Layer all the ingredients but the plant-based milk in a quart mason jar or a dish with a cover. Add ¼ cup (60 ml) of the milk. Stirring the milk in will give you the room needed to add the other ¼ cup (60 ml) of milk. Mix well and let sit in the fridge overnight. Stir and eat.

PER RECIPE: Calories 205.5, protein 20.0 g, total fat 3.8 g, carbohydrates 22.1 g, sodium 107.1 mg, fiber 4.5 g

COCONUT CREAM OVERNIGHT REFRIGERATOR OATMEAL

GLUTEN-FREE, SOY-FREE, OIL-FREE

Hot oatmeal is not what I crave in the summer months. However, I never give up oatmeal completely; I love a sweet, cooling breakfast that's ready to grab on my way to work. These no-cook overnight oats are like eating the filling of a coconut cream pie!

MAKES 1 SERVING

⅓ cup (31 g) rolled oats

1 tablespoon (10 g) chia seeds

1 (6 oz [170 g]) container of coconut flavored vegan yogurt, or ¾ cup (170 g) plain vegan yogurt and ¼ teaspoon coconut extract

⅓ cup (79 ml) coconut flavored almond milk, or plain plant-based milk and ¼ teaspoon coconut extract

2 tablespoons (12 g) shredded coconut

sweetener to taste, optional (if using plain yogurt and milk, you may need to use this)

Layer all the ingredients in a quart mason jar or a dish with a cover. Mix well and let sit in the fridge overnight. Stir and eat.

PER RECIPE: Calories 381.0, protein 8.0 g, total fat 20.6 g, carbohydrates 51.2 g, sodium 76.6 mg, fiber 9.5 g

CINNAMON ROLL OVERNIGHT OATS

GLUTEN-FREE, SOY-FREE, OIL-FREE

I think about breakfast before I go to bed. It's like looking into a crystal ball and predicting what perfect flavor will start off my day. The flavor of cinnamon rolls, even in cold oats, is the best way to start out a long, stressful day. This is a healthy cinnamon roll version that you can have any old time.

MAKES 1 SERVING

⅔ cup (177 ml) vanilla nondairy milk (or plain plus ½ teaspoon vanilla)

⅓ cup (31 g) rolled oats

1 (6 oz [170 g]) container vegan yogurt

½ teaspoon cinnamon

⅛ teaspoon allspice

1 tablespoon (14 g) chopped pecans or walnuts, optional

Combine all the ingredients except for the walnuts or pecans in a mason jar or a dish with a cover. Mix well and let sit in the fridge overnight. Stir, top with nuts and eat.

PER RECIPE: Calories 400.9, protein 7.1 g, total fat 19.0 g, carbohydrates 52.5 g, sodium 104.7 mg, fiber 6.3 g

PETITE PORTION BANANA PUDDING OVERNIGHT OATS

This may be a smaller portion, but it still packs a big flavorful punch with sweet bananas in a creamy vanilla yogurt "pudding." If you have some vegan vanilla wafers on hand, crush one or two and sprinkle it over the top for a real Southern banana pudding.

MAKES 1 SERVING

1 medium banana

¼ teaspoon lemon juice

¼ cup (57 g) vegan based yogurt

½ teaspoon vanilla

¼ cup (20 g) oats

sweetener of choice, to taste if needed

Mash the banana in a small bowl with the lemon juice, yogurt and vanilla. Mix in oats and sweetener and then transfer to a pint mason jar or a small container with a lid. Let sit in the fridge overnight. Stir and eat.

PER RECIPE: Calories 242.5, protein 4.1 g, total fat 2.9 g, carbohydrates 51.0 g, sodium 20.3 mg, fiber 6.1 g

BLUEBERRY EARL GREY OVERNIGHT REFRIGERATOR OATS (NO YOGURT)

GLUTEN-FREE, SOY-FREE, OIL-FREE

I drink tea of all kinds, but Earl Grey is my absolute favorite with its bergamot orange aroma and flavor. I love it with vanilla nondairy milk and think it goes great with blueberries, so I knew that this oatmeal would be one of my favorites. You can add a teaspoon or two of chia seeds to make this extra thick.

MAKES 1 SERVING

⅔ cup (177 ml) vanilla nondairy milk

1 teaspoon Earl Grey tea in a tea ball (or 1 tea bag)

⅔ cup (98 g) blueberries

⅓ cup (31g) rolled oats

1 tablespoon (15 ml) agave nectar, or sweetener of choice, to taste

Heat the milk until very hot but not boiling, then steep tea for 4 minutes. Once you discard the tea, you are left with Earl Grey flavored milk! Add all the remaining ingredients in a mason jar or a dish with a cover. Mix well and let sit in the fridge overnight. Stir and eat.

PER SERVING: Calories 273.4, protein 4.7 g, total fat 3.7 g, carbohydrates 58.2 g, sodium 105.2 mg, fiber 5.9 g

Add in ¼ teaspoon ground culinary lavender or ⅛ teaspoon lavender extract to make even more delightful.

BLACKBERRY MOJITO OVERNIGHT REFRIGERATOR OATS (NO YOGURT)

Sweet juicy blackberries soaked in bright lime and mint flavors with the faintest aroma of rum will perk you up even on the toughest mornings. You can add a teaspoon or two of chia seeds to make this extra thick.

MAKES 1 SERVING

1 cup (165 g) blackberries (cut in half if large)

½ cup (120 ml) unsweetened nondairy milk

⅓ cup (31 g) rolled oats

2 tablespoons (30 g) minced fresh mint or ⅛ teaspoon mint extract

zest from ½ lime or ¼ teaspoon lime oil

½ teaspoon rum or rum extract, optional

1 tablespoon (15 ml) agave, to taste (or your choice of sweetener, to taste)

Combine all the ingredients in a mason jar or a dish with a cover. Mix well and let sit in the fridge overnight. Stir and eat.

PER RECIPE: Calories 255.8, protein 4.8 g, total fat 4.3 g, carbohydrates 52.9 g, sodium 90.0 mg, fiber 10.8 g

STRAWBERRIES AND CREAM OVERNIGHT REFRIGERATOR OATS (NO YOGURT)

This can be made with frozen strawberries in the dead of winter and give you a moment's break from the snow. It is great with the first strawberries of spring and every day in between the two seasons. You can add a teaspoon or two of chia seeds to make this extra thick.

MAKES 1 SERVING

⅔ cup (177 ml) vanilla nondairy milk (or plain plus ½ teaspoon vanilla)

⅓ cup (31 g) rolled oats

¼ cup (42 g) minced strawberries (fresh or frozen)

2 tablespoons (40 g) strawberry fruit-sweetened jam

¼ teaspoon vanilla

sweetener of choice, to taste (you may not need any if the strawberries are sweet)

Combine all the ingredients in a mason jar or a dish with a cover. Mix well and let sit in the fridge overnight. Stir and eat.

PER RECIPE: Calories 280, protein 4.3 g, total fat 3.9 g, carbohydrates 58.8 g, sodium 100.1 mg, fiber 4.7 g

CHOCOLATE CHERRY OVERNIGHT REFRIGERATOR OATS (NO YOGURT)

GLUTEN-FREE, SOY-FREE, OIL-FREE

Send this decadent breakfast off with a loved one for Valentine's Day or really any day you want to pack some extra love for them to take to work or school. This oatmeal is rich with chocolate and has little bursts of bright cherry flavor. You can add a teaspoon or two of chia seeds to make this extra thick.

MAKES 1 SERVING

⅔ cup (177 ml) vanilla nondairy milk

⅓ cup (31 g) rolled oats

½ cup (77 g) minced pitted cherries

1½ tablespoons (22 g) mini chocolate chips

Combine all the ingredients in a mason jar or a dish with a cover. Mix well and let sit in the fridge overnight. Stir and eat.

PER RECIPE: Calories 324.6, protein 6.0 g, total fat 11.0 g, carbohydrates 56.1 g, sodium 99.5 mg, fiber 5.3 g

CARROT CAKE SMOOTHIE

GLUTEN-FREE, SOY-FREE, OIL-FREE

Smoothies are a great way to pack in some flavor and nutrition for an on-the-go breakfast. I vary the ingredients based on what I have on hand or to suit my mood. Don't have vanilla yogurt or milk? Just add ½ teaspoon of vanilla extract. Use your favorite sweetener so that it fits into your eating plan. I sometimes use a monk fruit powder that I like.

MAKES 2 SERVINGS

1 cup (227 ml) unsweetened vanilla nondairy milk

½ cup (114 g) vanilla nondairy yogurt

⅓ cup (82 g) pineapple chunks

¼ cup (24 g) rolled oats

2 medium carrots, shredded

1 tablespoon (14 g) walnuts

1 tablespoon (12 g) shredded coconut

sweetener of choice, to taste

¼ to ½ cup (118 g) crushed ice, optional

Add the milk, yogurt, pineapple, oats, carrots, walnuts and coconut to a blender and blend until mostly smooth—there will still be tiny pieces of carrots and coconut that will add a nice texture, so don't worry if it's not perfectly smooth.

Taste and add your favorite sweetener if needed. I find the sweetness in the vanilla yogurt enough for me, but you could also use sweetened nondairy milk instead of or in addition to a sweetener.

Add in some crushed ice and blend again if you want to make a colder and thicker smoothie.

PER SERVING: Calories 270.6, protein 4.5 g, total fat 12.5 g, carbohydrates 38.0 g, sodium 145.9 mg, fiber 5.6 g

GREEN OAT SMOOTHIE

I like to make my smoothies thick with frozen fruit, but if you prefer a thinner smoothie, you can use all fresh fruit or use a little more liquid. If you're new to green smoothies, kale and spinach are very mild, as is lettuce. Work your way up to Swiss chard, collards and beyond. I like to grow some greens in containers outside and snip a handful in the spring and fall.

MAKES 2 SERVINGS

¼ cup (24 g) rolled oats

1½ cups (354 ml) nondairy milk

½ to 1 cup (67 g) kale or spinach (fresh or frozen)

1 to 2 cups (460 g) assorted frozen fruit (berries, mango, pineapple, etc.)

sweetener, to taste (I use ¼ teaspoon stevia plus 1 teaspoon agave nectar)

Add the oats and milk to your blender and blend until smooth. Add the greens and do the same. Now add in the fruit and sweetener and blend until smooth. You may need to add some extra liquid as you go depending on the strength of your blender.

PER SERVING: Calories 185.7, protein 3.2 g, total fat 4.8 g, carbohydrates 32.7 g, sodium 26.2 mg, fiber 4.3 g

You can always throw in some protein powder or Vitamin C to personalize your smoothie!

POMEGRANATE ROSE SMOOTHIE

GLUTEN-FREE, SOY-FREE, OIL-FREE

I love the flavor of rose in foods. It pairs perfectly with the pomegranate in this breakfast and elevates this to a "special occasion" smoothie. If you are not a fan of rose, you can always just leave it out!

MAKES 2 SERVINGS

2 cups (200 ml) pomegranate juice

1½ cups (345 g) frozen blueberries

½ cup (48 g) rolled oats

½ cup (118 ml) nondairy milk

½ cup (113 g) nondairy yogurt

1 teaspoon rosewater or to taste

sweetener, to taste (I use ¼ teaspoon stevia)

Add all the ingredients to your blender and blend until smooth. If you are new to rosewater, add ½ teaspoon first and taste it. If it's not strong enough add the other ½ teaspoon.

Remember, you can always throw in some protein powder or Vitamin C to personalize your smoothie!

PER SERVING: Calories 416.1, protein 5.3 g, total fat 3.4 g, carbohydrates 89.4 g, sodium 98.3 mg, fiber 8.7 g

CHAI-SPICED OAT SHAKE

GLUTEN-FREE, SOY-FREE, OIL-FREE

You can keep this caffeine-free or add in your morning coffee or tea to make an all-in-one breakfast that you can drink in your car. This shake is thinner than the smoothies, but if you use a frozen banana in place of a fresh one, it will be a little thicker.

MAKES 2 CUPS (473 ML)

¼ cup (24 g) rolled oats

½ banana

1 cup (237 ml) nondairy milk, tea or coffee

¼ teaspoon stevia plus 1 teaspoon agave nectar (or sweetener of choice, to taste)

¼ teaspoon cinnamon

⅛ teaspoon cardamom

¹⁄₁₆ teaspoon nutmeg

pinch allspice

pinch cloves

⅛ teaspoon xanthan gum or ¼ teaspoon pectin

½ to 1 cup (118 to 235 g) ice (crushed if possible)

Add the oats, nondairy milk, sweeteners and spices to a blender and blend well.

Add the xanthan gum or pectin and blend for about a minute to get it well incorporated. This is what will help hold everything together, so don't leave it out!

Now add the ice and blend well. If you don't have a powerful blender, add it a little at a time. If you have a powerful blender, add ½ to 1 cup (118 to 235 g) of ice and blend the shake into an ice cream.

PER CUP: Calories 91.4, protein 2.3 g, total fat 2.6 g, carbohydrates 17.2 g, sodium 97.4 mg, fiber 2.4 g

CHAPTER FOUR

GRANOLAS AND BARS FOR BREAKFAST AND BEYOND

I love granola and the fact that it's so easy to make. Feel free to alter the recipes by using the sweeteners that you like. Flavors like chocolate hazelnut, bourbon pecan and pumpkin raisin feel more like a treat than breakfast and are just the thing to fuel your day.

If you don't even have time to pour some nondairy milk over a bowl of granola, you can grab a bar to eat on the go. They are easy to make on the weekend, and you can stash a few in the freezer if you won't eat the whole batch fast enough.

The crunchy texture of granola lends itself to savory flavors, too. Make sure to try sun-dried tomato granola on your next vegan Caesar salad to add some flavor and a little crunch. Curry cashew granola can be put on top of a casserole or even a plain nondairy yogurt for an Indian twist to breakfast.

If you are following an oil-free diet, you can leave out the coconut oil from the granolas. Just know that they won't clump up when you cook them.

CHOCOLATE HAZELNUT GRANOLA

GLUTEN-FREE, SOY-FREE

Chocolate in the morning seems so indulgent, but this granola is full of healthy oats, flaxseed and hazelnuts so there's no need to feel guilty. This is great sprinkled over coconut milk yogurt and reminds me of a hazelnut chocolate spread, such as Nutella.

MAKES ABOUT 3 CUPS (241 GRAMS)

⅓ cup (80 ml) maple syrup or agave nectar

¼ cup (52 g) coconut oil (refined or unrefined), melted

2 cups (184 g) rolled oats

1 cup (115 g) chopped hazelnuts

⅓ cup (29 g) cocoa

2 tablespoons (14 g) ground flax

½ teaspoon vanilla extract

⅛ teaspoon salt, optional

Preheat the oven to 350°F (177°C). If your maple syrup is cold, warm it with the coconut oil before mixing. Mix all of the ingredients together in a mixing bowl. Spread on a cookie sheet that is either lightly sprayed with oil or on a cookie sheet lined with parchment paper.

Bake for 20 to 25 minutes, but keep an eye on it and stir every 5 to 10 minutes. In the oven, your granola can go from not done to overdone quickly!

Let cool on the cookie sheet and store in an airtight jar.

PER ¼ cup serving: Calories 184, protein 3.8 g, total fat 12.1 g, carbohydrates 18.2 g, sodium 25.0 mg, fiber 3.4 g

{ Recipe variation: Add ½ cup (90 g) mini chocolate chips after the granola is cooled to make it extra decadent. }

BOURBON-SCENTED PECAN GRANOLA

This is a unique granola. In addition to the traditional rolled oats, it uses steel-cut oats and a hint of bourbon to add that extra Southern twist. You can leave out the bourbon or use rum or brandy extract instead.

MAKES ABOUT 2½ CUPS (201 GRAMS)

1½ cups (140 g) rolled oats

½ cup (40 g) steel-cut oats

½ cup (54 g) minced pecans

¼ cup (60 ml) agave nectar

¼ cup (52 ml) coconut oil (refined or unrefined), melted

1 to 2 teaspoons (5-10 ml) bourbon, to taste

1 teaspoon vanilla extract

Preheat the oven to 350°F (177°C). Mix all of the ingredients together in a mixing bowl. Spread on a cookie sheet that is either lightly sprayed with oil or on a cookie sheet lined with parchment paper.

Bake for 20 to 25 minutes, but keep an eye on the granola and stir every 5 to 10 minutes because in the oven your granola can go from not done to overdone very quickly! Let the granola cool on the cookie sheet and store in an airtight container.

PER ¼ CUP (40 G) SERVING: Calories 183.3, protein 3.2 g, total fat 11 g, carbohydrates 19.1 g, sodium 0.0 mg, fiber 2.5 g

{ You can use all rolled oats if you aren't up to braving the extra crunchy steel-cut oats. }

FAT–FREE PUMPKIN RAISIN GRANOLA

GLUTEN–FREE, SOY–FREE, OIL–FREE

This granola is soy-free, oil-free and nut-free so it works for most allergies. Pumpkin is also good for replacing fat when making cookies, cakes and granola bars.

MAKES ABOUT 2½ CUPS (201 GRAMS)

2 cups (184 g) rolled oats

½ cup (122 g) pumpkin purée

¼ cup (41.25 g) raisins

¼ cup (36.25 g) coconut sugar or brown sugar, or more to suit your taste

¼ cup (60 ml) agave nectar or ½ teaspoon stevia

1 tablespoon (7 g) chia or flaxseeds

1 teaspoon cinnamon

½ teaspoon allspice

pinch of cloves

salt, to taste

Preheat the oven to 350°F (177°C). Mix all of the ingredients together in a mixing bowl. Spread on a parchment paper lined cookie sheet.

Cook for 25 to 35 minutes, but keep an eye on it and stir every 10 minutes because in the oven your granola can go from not ready to overdone very quickly! Let the granola cool on the cookie sheet and store it in an airtight container.

PER ¼ CUP (40 G) SERVING: Calories 128, protein 2.5 g, total fat 1.7 g, carbohydrates 29.3 g, sodium 3 mg, fiber 2.6 g

SUN-DRIED TOMATO AND KALAMATA OLIVE SAVORY GRANOLA

SOY-FREE, GLUTEN-FREE OPTION*, OIL-FREE OPTION**

The bursts of sun-dried tomato and olives in this granola are a delightful surprise on top of a salad or pasta. You could also just eat it on plain yogurt, which could serve as a great lunch!

MAKES 2 CUPS (160 GRAMS)

2 tablespoons (14 g) ground flaxseed mixed with 4 tablespoons (60 ml) warm water

1 cup (92 g) rolled oats (*make sure oats are marked gluten-free)

2 tablespoons (30 ml) olive oil (**replace oil with 1 tablespoon [15 g] ground flaxseed mixed with 2 tablespoons [30 ml] warm water in addition to the amount above)

2 tablespoons (14 g) minced sun-dried tomatoes

2 tablespoons (17 g) minced Kalamata olives

1 teaspoon dried oregano

½ teaspoon dried basil

⅛ teaspoon ground rosemary

⅛ teaspoon granulated garlic

salt, to taste

Preheat oven to 350°F (177°C) and either oil a cookie sheet or line it with parchment paper.

Add all ingredients but the salt to a medium-sized mixing bowl. Mix well, then add salt to taste.

Pour the mixture onto the prepared cookie sheet and press thin. You should have one large, flat piece of granola that is about ¼-inch (0.6-cm thin). Bake for 20 to 25 minutes, until the edges are browned and the middle is no longer wet.

Let cool on the cookie sheet and break it up into large or small chunks with your hands. Use to top salads or pasta, or just eat by the handful for a snack!

PER ¼ CUP (40 G) SERVING: Calories 61, protein 2 g, total fat 3 g, carbohydrates 8 g, sodium 45.0 mg, fiber 2 g

{ Reduce the olive oil to 1 tablespoon (15 ml) if your Kalamata olives are packed in oil. }

PEPITA SUNFLOWER SEED SAVORY GRANOLA

SOY-FREE, GLUTEN-FREE OPTION*, OIL-FREE OPTION**

The cumin and chili powder gives this savory granola a Mexican twist. Sprinkle this on top of a taco salad, bake on top of an enchilada casserole or just eat by the handful for a snack!

MAKES 2½ CUPS (201 GRAMS)

2 tablespoons (14 g) ground flaxseed mixed with 4 tablespoons (60 g) warm water

1 cup (92 g) rolled oats (*make sure oats are marked gluten-free)

3 tablespoons (45 ml) olive oil (**replace oil with 1 tablespoon [15 g] ground flaxseed mixed with 2 tablespoons [30 ml] warm water in addition to the amount above)

½ cup (69 g) roasted pepitas (pumpkin seeds)

½ cup (70 g) sunflower seeds

1 tablespoon (5 g) oregano

1 teaspoon cumin

½ teaspoon smoked paprika

¼ teaspoon chili powder

⅛ teaspoon granulated garlic

salt, to taste (will vary if using unsalted seeds or salted seeds)

Preheat oven to 350°F (177°C) and either oil a cookie sheet or line it with parchment paper.

Add all ingredients but the salt to a medium-sized mixing bowl. Mix well, then add salt to taste.

Pour the mixture onto the prepared cookie sheet and press thin. You should have one large, flat piece of granola that is about ¼ to ⅛-inch thin. Bake for 20 to 25 minutes, until the edges are browned and the middle is no longer wet.

Let cool on cookie sheet and break it up into large or small chunks with your hands.

PER ¼ CUP (40 G) SERVING: Calories 124.3, protein 3 g, total fat 8.7 g, carbohydrates 9 g, sodium 18 mg, fiber 2.3 g

CURRY CASHEW SAVORY GRANOLA

One of the reasons I love curry is that it blends spices used in desserts with savory and fiery flavors. Because of that, this granola straddles the line between savory and sweet. Try it as a delicious topping to the Indian-Spiced Tomato Soup (recipe on page 107) or a great change of pace to your normal morning yogurt.

MAKES 2 CUPS (161 GRAMS)

2 tablespoons (14 g) ground flaxseed mixed with 4 tablespoons (59 ml) warm water

1 cup (92 g) rolled oats (*make sure oats are marked gluten-free)

3 tablespoons (45 ml) olive oil (**replace oil with 1 tablespoon [15 g] ground flaxseed mixed with 2 tablespoons [30 ml] warm water in addition to the amount above)

⅓ cup (55 g) golden raisins

⅓ cup (26 g) finely shredded coconut

⅓ cup (43 g) minced cashews nuts

1 teaspoon garam masala

½ teaspoon cumin

¼ teaspoon granulated garlic

¼ teaspoon chili powder

¼ teaspoon ground coriander

⅛ teaspoon ground mustard

salt, to taste

Preheat oven to 350°F (177°C) and either oil a cookie sheet or line it with parchment paper.

Add all ingredients but the salt to a medium-sized mixing bowl. Mix well, then add salt to taste.

Pour the mixture onto the prepared cookie sheet and press thin. You should have one large, flat piece about ¼ to ⅛-inch thin. Bake for 20 to 25 minutes, until the edges are browned and the middle is no longer wet.

Let cool on cookie sheet and break it up into large or small chunks with your hands. Use to top salads or plain yogurt, or just eat by the handful for a snack!

PER ¼ CUP SERVING: Calories 165.7 , protein 3 g, total fat 11.1 g, carbohydrates 15 g, sodium 3.4 mg, fiber 2 g

PEANUT BUTTER BANANA GRANOLA BARS

SOY-FREE, GLUTEN-FREE, OIL-FREE

With filling banana and peanut butter, these bars will keep you going all morning long. Plus it's always a better morning if chocolate is involved!

MAKES ABOUT 14 SMALL BARS

1 medium ripe banana

½ cup (129 g) peanut butter

¼ cup (60 ml) agave nectar or maple syrup

2 tablespoons (14 g) ground flaxseeds mixed with 4 tablespoons (60 ml) warm water

3 cups (276 g) rolled oats

½ cup (120 g) vegan chocolate chips, optional

¼ teaspoon salt (if using unsalted peanut butter)

Preheat oven to 350°F (177°C). Tear a piece of parchment paper to cover a small baking sheet. Set aside for later.

In a medium mixing bowl, mash the banana and then mix in the peanut butter, agave nectar and flax mixture until smooth. Add in the oats and keep mixing until it's well combined. Stir in the optional chocolate chips.

Scrape mixture onto the middle of the baking sheet lined with parchment paper and form the mixture into a rectangle. It will be very sticky, so push the edges together with a spatula.

Bake for 20 to 25 minutes or until the bottom begins to brown. Let cool, then cut into small rectangles.

PER SMALL BAR: Calories 194.0, protein 5.3 g, total fat 8.5 g, carbohydrates 25.8 g, sodium 34.4 mg, fiber 3.6 g

NO-BAKE CARDAMOM CHERRY GRANOLA BARS

GLUTEN-FREE, SOY-FREE, OIL-FREE

You can make these no-bake granola bars when it's too hot to use the oven. Cardamom is a wonderful spice for sweets, and it is perfect with the tartness of the dried cherries. Eating them will keep you cool, too, since you'll be grabbing these bars straight from the fridge.

MAKES 12 BARS

1 cup (237 ml) water

2 tablespoons (14 g) ground flaxseed or chia seeds

15 dates

½ teaspoon vanilla

½ teaspoon ground cardamom

2 cups (184 g) rolled oats

1½ cups (48 g) puffed brown rice cereal

½ cup (80 g) diced dried cherries

Line a 10" x 8" (25.5 x 20-cm) pan with wax paper and set aside. Blend the water, flaxseed, dates, vanilla and cardamom until smooth. If you have a less powerful blender and have a few pieces of dates, that's okay.

Mix the oats, rice cereal and cherries in a mixing bowl and pour the date mixture over it. Mix well. Scrape this mixture onto the prepared pan and spread evenly. Cover with another piece of wax paper and mash the mixture using the wax paper to keep it from sticking to your hands.

Refrigerate overnight. In the morning, holding onto the bottom layer of wax paper, remove the chilled mixture and set on a cutting board. Cut into 12 bars. You can leave them on the wax paper you used or wrap the bars up in groups or individual bars. Store in the fridge.

PER BAR: Calories 110.8, protein 2.4 g, total fat 1.4 g, carbohydrates 23.2 g, sodium 1.5 mg, fiber 2.9 g

NUT AND FRUIT GRANOLA BARS

SOY-FREE, GLUTEN-FREE, OIL-FREE

Full of crunchy nuts and sweet dried fruit, this granola bar has it all, except added oil! These bars are so much fun to make and are a great way to use up the last bits and pieces of chopped nuts and dried fruit you have on hand. It even has pumpkin! My favorite combination is an assortment with peanuts and fancy nuts, plus a mix of dried berries. I use salted nuts and love how you get a mix of sweet and salty in every bite.

MAKES 12 BARS

2 tablespoons (14 g) ground flaxseeds mixed with 4 tablespoons (59 ml) warm water

1 cup (245 g) pumpkin purée

2 cups (184 g) rolled oats

1 cup (92 g) chopped nuts

1 cup (160 g) dried fruit (chopped if large fruit, or whole if raisins or berries)

¼ teaspoon salt (if using unsalted nuts)

Preheat oven to 350°F (177°C). Line a 10" x 8" (25.5 x 20-cm) pan with parchment paper or spray the pan with oil.

Mix all the ingredients together until combined, then scrape the mixture into the pan and press in well. Score into 12 pieces, then bake for 20 to 25 minutes or until the edges begin to brown.

PER BAR: Calories 161.9, protein 3.4 g, total fat 8.0 g, carbohydrates 20.4 g, sodium 5.8 mg, fiber 4.4 g

PEPITA OATMEAL RAISIN COOKIE BARS

SOY-FREE

Bar cookies are so much fun to make, but honestly I get tired of brownies and blondies. Somer McCowan's cookie bars have the cinnamon and raisin flavors you've come to love in oatmeal cookies, but in an easy one-pan dish. Somer also includes pepitas, also known as pumpkin seeds, to give them an earthier flare. She blogs at VedgedOut.com. She came up with these for her husband on Valentine's Day because in addition to being talented, she's nice!

MAKES 16 SQUARES

DRY INGREDIENTS

2 cups (264 g) whole wheat pastry flour

1 cup (92 g) rolled oats

1 cup (200 g) organic sugar

1 cup (165 g) raisins

1 cup (138 g) pumpkin seeds (pepitas)

1 teaspoon salt

1 teaspoon baking powder

2 teaspoons (5 g) ground cinnamon

WET INGREDIENTS

1 tablespoon (15 g) ground golden flaxseeds mixed with 3 tablespoons (45 ml) warm water

¾ cup (178 ml) nondairy milk

⅓ cup (70 ml) coconut oil, melted

2 teaspoons (10 ml) Mexican vanilla

Preheat oven to 350°F (177°C) and place parchment paper into a 9" x 13" (23 x 33-cm) baking dish (or spray with oil). Combine the dry ingredients in a large mixing bowl. Mix well, then stir in the wet ingredients.

Press dough into the prepared baking dish. Bake for 30 to 35 minutes on a lower rack in the oven so that the top doesn't get overly browned. Let cool for 5 to 10 minutes before slicing into bars and serving. This way, they will crumble less.

PER SQUARE: Calories 250.8, protein 5.1 g, total fat 9.6 g, carbohydrates 36.6 g, sodium 112.7 mg, fiber 4.1 g

{ If your Valentine prefers dark chocolate chips and chopped pecans to raisins and pepita seeds, go ahead and swap them out. I won't tell. —Love, Somer }

CHAPTER FIVE

SATISFYING SOUPS AND STEWS

Soups and stews may not be the first things that come to mind when you think of oats or oatmeal. However, these easy and soul-satisfying recipes are bound to change the way you think and—even better—they will change how you eat!

In my Virtuous Carrot-Herb Oatmeal Soup and the Mushroom Ginger Congee, rolled oats are used as a nutritious thickener. Rolled oats can do even more, however; in the Creamy Butternut Squash Oat Soup, they help you mimic a cream-based soup by disappearing once you purée the ingredients together. This way, no one will know your healthy secret!

It's about time to see steel-cut oats outside of the breakfast bowl. Remember, it's just another delicious grain like barley or rice and it adds a great texture and make the dish heartier. You'll really enjoy it in the Scottish-Inspired Mushroom Lentil Stew.

The often overlooked whole oat groats will be a delightful addition to your pantry. They add a chewy texture, and their long-cooking needs pair perfectly with a slow cooker. Enjoy the ease and your day away from the stove with Slow Cooker Black Bean Oat Groat Soup and Slow Cooker Creole Red Bean Quinoa Oat Groats.

CHICKPEA VEGGIE SOUP

GLUTEN-FREE, SOY-FREE, OIL-FREE OPTION*

This healthy soup tastes like you slaved over a hot stove all day but comes together fast enough to eat any weeknight. Sweet potatoes, carrots and kale make this delicious. Using steel-cut oats as your grain of choice makes the soup thick and hearty too!

MAKES 8 SERVINGS

2 tablespoons (30 ml) olive oil
(*use broth or water instead)

¼ cup (50 g) minced onion

3 cloves garlic, minced

1½ cups (270 g) diced sweet potato

1 cup (110 g) chopped carrots

1 can (15 oz [425 g]) chickpeas

6 cups (1420 ml) water

½ cup (40 g) steel-cut oats

4 tablespoons (24 g) nutritional yeast, divided

1 teaspoon marjoram

½ teaspoon smoked paprika

½ teaspoon basil

¼ teaspoon thyme

¼ teaspoon ground rosemary

1½ cups (270 g) chopped kale or other green like chard or collards

salt and pepper, to taste

Add the olive oil to a soup pot and heat over medium heat. Once hot, add onions and sauté for about 5 minutes, until translucent. Then add the garlic and cook for 3 more minutes.

Add the sweet potato, carrots, chickpeas and water, then turn the heat to high and bring to a boil.

Once the soup is boiling, turn to low and add the oats, 2 tablespoons (30 g) of the nutritional yeast, marjoram, smoked paprika, basil, thyme and ground rosemary. Cover and simmer until the oats are thoroughly cooked, about 20 to 25 minutes.

Add in the kale and the other 2 tablespoons (30 g) of nutritional yeast. Cook about 5 to 10 minutes until the kale is tender. Add salt and pepper to taste before serving.

PER SERVING: Calories 177.6, protein 8.1 g, total fat 5.3 g, carbohydrates 24.2 g, sodium 41.9 mg, fiber 6.1 g

CREAMY BUTTERNUT SQUASH OAT SOUP

GLUTEN-FREE, SOY-FREE, OIL-FREE OPTION*

Oats thicken this winter squash soup and once puréed, create the creamy texture. You can use any winter squash in place of the butternut or use that can of pumpkin you have hiding in your pantry. In fact, even carrots would work in a pinch!

MAKES 4 SERVINGS

2 tablespoons (30 ml) olive oil (*use broth or water instead)

¼ cup (50 g) minced onion

2 cloves garlic, minced

1 teaspoon garam masala

⅛ teaspoon cayenne powder

2 cups (473 ml) unsweetened nondairy milk

½ cup (48 g) rolled oats

1½ cups (425 g) butternut squash purée

1 cup (237 ml) water

salt and pepper, to taste

Heat olive oil in a soup pot over medium heat. Once hot, add onions and sauté about 5 minutes until translucent. Then add the garlic and cook for 3 more minutes.

Add the garam masala, cayenne, nondairy milk, rolled oats, butternut squash and water. Bring to a boil, then cover and lower the heat. Let simmer on low heat for 10 to 20 minutes until the oats are tender.

Carefully pour the soup into a blender to purée, or use an immersion blender in the pot. Purée until smooth, then add salt and pepper to taste.

PER SERVING: Calories 181.4, protein 3.8 g, total fat 9.3 g, carbohydrates 21.7 g, sodium 91.3mg, fiber 3.5 g

Try this creamy rolled oat trick on your favorite cream-of soup.
It works great with broccoli, cauliflower or even spinach.

SLOW COOKER BLACK BEAN OAT GROAT SOUP

GLUTEN-FREE, SOY-FREE, OIL-FREE

You know I can't keep my slow cooker out of the picture for long. Oat groats are perfect for slow cooking because they take so much longer to cook than steel-cut oats. In case you were wondering, oat groats are whole oats with just the hull removed. They go great as the grain of choice in this Mexican-spiced soup.

MAKES 6 SERVINGS

MORNING INGREDIENTS

8 cups (1,893 ml) water

1½ cups (302 g) dry black beans

1 cup (110 g) chopped carrots

½ cup (92 g) oat groats

6 cloves garlic, minced

3 vegetable bouillon cubes

2 bay leaves

1 teaspoon cumin

1 teaspoon smoked paprika

1 teaspoon chili powder (increase to 2 or 3 if you like things spicy)

EVENING INGREDIENTS

1 (28 oz [793 g]) can crushed tomatoes

additional 1 teaspoon cumin

salt and pepper, to taste

TOPPINGS

chopped cilantro

vegan sour cream or cashew cream

diced avocado —

squeeze of lime

In the morning: Add all the morning ingredients to a 4-to 5-quart slow cooker and cook on low for 8 to 10 hours.

In the evening: Turn the slow cooker to high and add the tomatoes and extra cumin. Cook for about 30 minutes to 1 hour or until the soup is hot. If the tomatoes are room temperature, this won't take very long.

Before serving, add salt and pepper to taste. Either put a few of the toppings on each bowl of soup before serving or put out little bowls of toppings to let each person add their favorites.

PER SERVING: Calories 173.2, protein 11.7 g, total fat 0.9 g, carbohydrates 42.7 g, sodium 295.2mg, fiber 21.6 g

{ If you don't have a slow cooker, soak the beans and oat groats overnight and cook on the stove if you're home in the afternoon. You may have to add a bit more water to it as it cooks, so be sure to keep an eye on it! }

INDIAN-SPICED TOMATO SOUP

GLUTEN-FREE, SOY-FREE, OIL-FREE

I developed the idea for this soup when I went to the grocery store in December and found a bag of heirloom tomatoes on the reduced produce shelf. They needed to be used right away, and I was in the mood for soup. Once puréed, the soup gets very creamy because of the cooked rolled oats. This tomato soup has hints of garlic, ginger and a few Indian spices and is very mild if you leave out the optional chili powder.

MAKES 4 SERVINGS

2 (14.5 oz [411 g]) cans or 3 cups (480 g) diced fresh tomatoes

1½ cups (355 ml) water

½ cup (48 g) rolled oats

1 bouillon cube

3 teaspoons (2 g) grated ginger

4 garlic cloves, minced

1½ teaspoons ground coriander

1 teaspoon ground cumin

½ teaspoon mustard powder

pinch chili powder, optional

salt and pepper, to taste

Cook all the ingredients except for the salt and pepper over high heat in a soup pot until just boiling. Turn to low, then cover and simmer for 20 minutes or until the oats are cooked well. The tomatoes should be cooked down.

Carefully pour the hot soup into a blender to purée, or use an immersion blender. Add salt and pepper to taste. Serve with the Easy Oat Roti (recipe on page 31).

PER SERVING: Calories 71.7, protein 3.0 g, total fat 1.4 g, carbohydrates 13.3 g, sodium 1.2 mg, fiber 1.1 g

{ Since leftovers will thicken in the fridge, run with it by tossing in some firm pressed tofu and serving it over some steamed basmati rice. It reminds Cheryl of her favorite Indian dish—tofu masala. }

VIRTUOUS CARROT–HERB OATMEAL SOUP

In my oatmeal research, I kept running across recipes for oatmeal soup. It seemed odd until I made this soup and realized how inexpensive and comforting it is. My version is full of rolled oats, carrots, rutabagas and herbs like thyme and rosemary.

MAKES 4 SERVINGS

5 cups (1,183 ml) water

1 cup (92 g) rolled oats

1 cup (110 g) chopped carrots

½ cup (75 g) peeled and chopped rutabaga

1 teaspoon dried thyme

⅛ teaspoon ground rosemary

3 tablespoons (18 g) nutritional yeast

salt and pepper, to taste

Add the water, oats, carrots, rutabaga, thyme and rosemary to a soup pot and bring to a boil.

Once it comes to a boil, turn the heat to low and cook for 10 to 15 minutes or until the root veggies are tender. Stir in the nutritional yeast, then add salt and pepper to taste.

PER SERVING: Calories 116.8, protein 5.9 g, total fat 1.8 g, carbohydrates 17.5 g, sodium 5.7mg, fiber 3.7 g

{ If you can't find rutabagas, or just don't like them, you may substitute with turnips or potatoes. }

SLOW COOKER CREOLE RED BEAN QUINOA OAT GROATS

SOY-FREE, GLUTEN-FREE, OIL-FREE OPTION*

This stew is flavored with bell pepper, garlic and Cajun spices. The flavor is reminiscent of a jambalaya but the texture is closer to a thick gumbo. Any way you look at it, a bold hearty stew is always welcome on the dinner table—especially if it practically makes itself.

MAKES 6 SERVINGS

2 tablespoons (30 ml) olive oil (*or use broth)

½ cup (100 g) minced onion

¾ cup (115 g) minced bell pepper

4 cloves garlic, minced

2 teaspoons (10 g) smoked paprika

2 teaspoons (10 g) marjoram

2 teaspoons (10 g) oregano

⅛ teaspoon allspice

2 bay leaves

½ teaspoon ground cayenne pepper or to taste

½ cup (92 g) oat groats

½ cup (87 g) quinoa, rinsed

1½ cup (375 g) small red beans (or kidney beans that have been boiled on the stove for 10 minutes)

7 cups (1,656 ml) water

2 bouillon cubes

salt and pepper, to taste

Heat the oil over medium heat in a sauté pan and add in the onion once it's hot. Cook for about 5 minutes or until translucent. Add in the bell pepper, garlic, paprika, marjoram, oregano and allspice, then cook for another 3 to 5 minutes or until the spices become fragrant.

Add the cooked mixture to a 4-quart slow cooker along with the oat groats, quinoa, red beans, water, bay leaf, cayenne pepper and bouillon cubes. Cook on low for 7 to 9 hours.

Stir well, as this may cook a little dry on the bottom or in the corners. Before serving, add salt and pepper to taste.

PER SERVING: Calories 254, protein 15.8 g, total fat 5.4 g, carbohydrates 55.7 g, sodium 46.3 mg, fiber 30.6 g

MUSHROOM GINGER CONGEE

SOY-FREE, GLUTEN-FREE, OIL-FREE

Served in a bowl, Congee is a thick Asian comfort food that can soothe a sore throat or just make you feel better after a bad day. This recipe makes enough for two but feel free to double or triple if you're feeding more or want to keep some in the fridge for the duration of your cold. The mushrooms and ginger are great for getting your immune system back on track.

MAKES 2 SERVINGS

3 cups (710 ml) vegetable or vegan chick'n broth

½ cup (48 g) rolled oats

½ cup (35 g) minced mushrooms (shiitakes are great)

¼ cup (27 g) minced carrot or sweet potato

1 tablespoon (6 g) grated ginger

1 teaspoon soy sauce

½ teaspoon rice wine vinegar

salt, to taste

hot pepper flakes, to taste

Bring the broth, oats, mushrooms and minced carrot or sweet potato to a boil in a medium pot. Lower the heat to medium-low and add in the ginger, soy sauce and vinegar. Cook for 15 to 20 minutes until the oats are cooked and the stew becomes thick.

Before serving, add salt to taste and spice with hot pepper flakes.

PER SERVING: Calories 140.4, protein 3.9 g, total fat 1.5 g, carbohydrates 29.0 g, sodium 1570 mg, fiber 2.5 g

{ Mushrooms are great for your immune system, and ginger helps calm an upset stomach, so try having a bowl the minute you find yourself feeling tired or a little under the weather. }

FRAGRANT YELLOW SPLIT PEA AND ROLLED OAT DAL

SOY-FREE, GLUTEN-FREE, OIL-FREE OPTION*

Lentils dressed up in Indian spices always work their way into my weekly menu plan. Once you have the spices on hand, dal is cheap and easy to make, and the leftovers freeze great. Look for the spices in Indian markets or your local health food store's bulk bins. That way you can try the spices in small amounts. The oats add a nice heft to this traditional dal.

MAKES 6 SERVINGS

2 tablespoons (30 ml) olive oil (*use broth or water instead)

1 teaspoon cumin seed

1 teaspoon coriander seed

1 teaspoon mustard seeds

½ teaspoon fenugreek seeds, optional

¼ teaspoon cinnamon

¼ teaspoon garam masala

½ cup (100 g) diced onions

1 cup (192 g) yellow split peas

½ cup (48 g) rolled oats

2 black cardamom pods, optional

5 cups (1,183 ml) water

salt and pepper, to taste

Heat the olive oil over medium heat in a soup pot. Sauté the cumin seeds, coriander seeds, mustard seeds, fenugreek seeds (if using), cinnamon and garam masala about 5 minutes until they become fragrant.

Add the onion and sauté about 5 minutes until translucent.

Add the split peas, oats, black cardamom pods and water. Bring to a boil, then turn heat to low. Cover and cook until the peas are soft, 45 to 60 minutes. Season with salt and pepper, to taste.

Serve over rice or with some vegan naan.

PER SERVING: Calories 156.8, protein 6.3 g, total fat 5.4 g, carbohydrates 21.0 g, sodium 0.5 mg, fiber 7.6 g

Add in a few handfuls of kale or another green to give this dal a nutritional boost. Minced greens can be added in the last 5 minutes of cooking.

FULL-OF-VEGGIES WHITE CHILI

SOY-FREE, GLUTEN-FREE, OIL-FREE OPTION*

This is not your ordinary white chili. It's packed with mushrooms, bell pepper and carrots. Plus tomatillos add a much needed tang. The cannellini beans and rolled oats make it a thick chili worthy of being the star of a meal.

MAKES 6 SERVINGS

2 tablespoons (30 ml) olive oil (*use water or veggie broth)

½ cup (100 g) minced onion

3 cloves garlic, minced

1½ cups (198 g) finely chopped tomatillos

1 cup (54 g) chopped mushrooms

½ cup (77 g) minced bell pepper

½ cup (54 g) finely chopped carrots

2 tablespoons (9 g) green chilies

1 tablespoon (6 g) oregano

1½ teaspoons (7 g) cumin

½ to 1½ teaspoons (2.5-7.5 g) chili powder

1 (15 oz [425 g]) can cannellini beans (or 1½ cups [300 g] homemade of any white bean)

2 cups (473 ml) veggie broth, chicken style (see sidebar for other options)

½ cup (48 g) rolled oats

salt and pepper, to taste

FOR TOPPING

chopped fresh cilantro

cashew cream or vegan sour cream

lime wedges

picked jalapeños

In a Dutch oven or soup pot, heat the oil over medium heat. Once warm, sauté the onion about 5 minutes until translucent. Add the garlic, tomatillos, mushrooms, bell pepper, carrots, green chilies, oregano, cumin and chili powder. Cover and cook for 20 minutes or until the tomatillos are soft.

Stir in the beans and broth, then turn the heat to high. Once it begins to boil, add in the oats, turn heat to low and cover. Cook for another 20 minutes. Before serving, add salt and pepper to taste. Remember if you are using a new brand of broth it may be saltier than the last one you used. Always taste and season accordingly.

Serve with an array of toppings that each person can add to their chili. I like to put toppings in little Pyrex dishes so that I can just cover what's left and keep them in the fridge!

PER SERVING: Calories 167, protein 6.0 g, total fat 5.4 g, carbohydrates 24.1 g, sodium 348.1 mg, fiber 2.8 g

{ Chicken-style vegan broth is just veggie broth with yeast extract—there's nothing in it from chicken. You can use plain veggie broth with 2 to 3 teaspoons (10 to 15 g) of nutritional yeast instead. You could also use water plus 1 bouillon cube or, if you're in a pinch, water with some nutritional yeast works too. Remember there are always options! }

SCOTTISH–INSPIRED MUSHROOM LENTIL STEW

GLUTEN-FREE, SOY-FREE, OIL-FREE OPTION*

Inspired by a traditional Scottish beef and oatmeal stew, I went off on my own to create a thick stew of steel-cut oats, lentils and mushroom spotted with turnips and carrots. Serve with a big green salad to round off the meal. I promise you, it's delicious!

MAKES 6 SERVINGS

2 tablespoons (30 ml) olive oil (*use broth or water)

½ cup (100 g) minced onions

2 cups (140 g) chopped mushrooms

2 bay leaves

4 cups (946 ml) water

2 bouillon cube

1 cup (150 g) peeled and diced turnip

½ cup (65 g) diced carrot

½ cup (96 g) dried lentils

½ cup (40 g) steel-cut oats

2 teaspoons (10 g) thyme

salt and pepper, to taste

In a Dutch oven or soup pot heat the oil over medium heat. Once warm, sauté the onion until translucent, then add the mushrooms and bay leaves. Cover and simmer for 10 minutes.

Add the water, bouillon cube, turnip, carrot, lentils, oats and thyme. Turn the heat to high and bring to a boil. Then lower heat to medium-low, cover and cook for 45 to 60 minutes or until the lentils are tender.

Add salt and pepper to taste before serving.

PER SERVING: Calories 119.1, protein 5.6 g, total fat 2.6 g, carbohydrates 19.6 g, sodium 318.3 mg, fiber 4.2 g

You can use any type of mushrooms that you like. Button mushrooms are usually the least expensive, but check out your local Asian market and see if you can get shiitake or oyster mushrooms cheap. The last time I was there, I found oyster mushrooms for under $6 a pound.

BISCUIT-TOPPED SOY CURL STEW

My picky eater loves pot pies of all kinds, so this recipe is especially for her. You start the stew and then make the biscuits while it's cooking. It's a one-pot meal that vaguely reminds me of frozen pot pies from my childhood. It has a rich base that really makes this dish come together.

MAKES 4 SERVINGS

2 tablespoons (30 ml) olive oil (*use water or broth)

½ cup (100 g) minced onion

3 cloves garlic, minced

1 cup (110 g) chopped carrots

1 cup (200 g) chopped rutabagas or potatoes

3 cups (710 ml) water

1½ cups (270 g) soy curls

½ cup (96 g) DIY Golden Gravy Mix (recipe on page 25)

1 teaspoon thyme

½ teaspoon marjoram

salt and pepper, to taste

½ recipe Southern-Style Oat Biscuit (recipe page 28)

Preheat the oven to 400°F (204°C). Heat the olive oil in a Dutch oven or deep iron skillet over medium heat. Sauté the onion until translucent (about 5 minutes), and then add the garlic, carrots and rutabagas for 3 minutes more.

Add the water and soy curls and bring to a boil, then turn heat to low and simmer about 15 to 20 minutes until the root veggies are tender and the soy curls are reconstituted. Make the biscuits while the stew is cooking.

Whisk in the gravy mix, thyme and marjoram, and then simmer about 15 minutes until the stew thickens. Top with the 4 uncooked biscuits. Bake about 20 minutes until the biscuits are cooked through. You can touch the top of the biscuit to test it for firmness.

PER SERVING: Calories 388.2, protein 14.9 g, total fat 20.7 g, carbohydrates 38.8 g, sodium 309.5 mg, fiber 10.6 g

- Go ahead and make the full recipe of Southern-Style Oat Biscuits. You'll use four of the biscuits on the stew, but if you bake the other four, you'll have them ready for breakfast in the morning.
- If you want to make this soy-free, use a can of chickpeas and cut the water down to 1 cup (237 ml).

STEEL-CUT OAT BEAN CHILI

GLUTEN-FREE, SOY-FREE, OIL-FREE

This is my new go-to chili. It has almost no hands-on prep, uses ingredients from the pantry and is great for leftovers too. The smoky flavor and hearty beans make it just as good in a big bowl with a few tortilla chips as tucked away in a taco or burrito.

MAKES 6 SERVINGS

2 cups (473 ml) water plus 1 veggie bouillon cube (or 2 cups [475 ml] veggie broth)

½ cup (40 g) steel-cut oats

1 tablespoon (15 g) oregano

2 teaspoons (10 g) ground cumin

1 teaspoon chili powder

3 cloves garlic, minced

1 (14.5 oz [406 g]) can kidney beans, drained and rinsed (or 1½ cups [300 g] homemade)

1 (14.5 oz [406 g]) can black beans, drained and rinsed (or 1½ cups [300 g] homemade)

1 (14.5 oz [406 g]) can diced tomatoes, regular or fire-roasted

1 cup (80 g) frozen corn, regular or fire-roasted

½ to 1 teaspoon liquid smoke, to taste

juice of ½ a lime

salt and pepper, to taste

Bring the water and bouillon to a boil in a soup pot. Add oats and lower to medium heat.

Cook uncovered for about 15 minutes or until the oats are tender and most of the liquid has been absorbed.

Stir in the oregano, cumin, garlic, kidney beans, black beans, tomatoes, corn and liquid smoke. Cover and cook over low heat for 20 minutes to allow the flavors to meld.

Before serving, add the juice of half a lime as well as salt and pepper, to taste.

PER SERVING: Calories 179.6, protein 9.0 g, total fat 1.5 g, carbohydrates 32.1 g, sodium 218.3 mg, fiber 7.7 g

CHAPTER SIX

SAVORY OATS FOR LUNCH AND DINNER

Though oats have been in savory dishes for a long time, when American food journalist and author Mark Bittman brought them back into the spotlight, the blogging world went wild. Well, I kind of went wild too. Oats were finally getting the respect they deserve.

Now's the time to think of oats as what they are—a simple whole grain. Usually the first thing people think of is a morning bowl of porridge. But once you shift your perspective, a whole new world of meal ideas opens up. For instance, imagine a nutritious risotto made with long cooking oat groats or steel-cut oats warming your house in a Dutch oven on a cold winter night. Then push the oat envelope even further with homemade potato-oat gnocchi, stir-fried oats and oat dosas, which are lacy crepes studded with cumin seeds and cilantro.

No one will turn their nose up at Not-from-a-Box Mac and Oat Chez, Eggplant Pizza Sliders or Burgers of Beany Goodness, so there are plenty of traditional family favorites too!

NOT-FROM-A-BOX MAC AND OAT CHEZ

SOY-FREE, GLUTEN-FREE OPTION*, OIL-FREE OPTION**

Cheryl, my grown-up picky eater, loves her boxed mac and chez, so it can be hard to get her into gourmet territory. If she's not interested in trying one of my experimental dinners, she always pulls a box of mac and chez out of the pantry. Now I have a much healthier and inexpensive option for her to eat, which makes me feel better.

MAKES 4 SERVINGS

½ pound (227 g) whole wheat elbow pasta (*use gluten-free pasta)

1 to 1½ cups (237 to 355 ml) unsweetened nondairy milk

½ cup (90 g) DIY Oat Chez Powder (see recipe page 24)

1 tablespoon (15 ml) vegan margarine or coconut oil, optional (**leave out to make oil-free)

½ teaspoon apple cider vinegar or ½ to 1 teaspoon prepared mustard (to add tang)

salt and pepper, to taste

Cook pasta according to package directions and pour into a strainer to drain when done.

Add 1 cup (235 ml) of the milk, chez powder, vegan margarine (if using) and apple cider vinegar to the pot that you just cooked the pasta in and turn the heat to medium. Whisk often until the sauce thickens up. If it gets a bit too thick, just add more milk.

Once it's thick, stir in the drained pasta and mix well. If the sauce seems too thick, you can add some more milk here too. Add salt and pepper to taste before serving.

PER SERVING: Calories 267.0, protein 10.0 g, total fat 4.8 g, carbohydrates 46.1 g, sodium 217.1 mg, fiber 6.0 g

{ Use snack-sized Ziploc bags to portion out the chez powder and put in mason jars with the elbow macaroni. If you include a card with the recipe, then you either have a gift or a ready-to-go recipe to store in your pantry. }

OATS-BURY STEAKS

SOY-FREE, GLUTEN-FREE, OIL-FREE

These patties combine beans, veggies and oats into something worthy of being the star of your dinner plate. The seasoning blend plus the mushrooms give this patty a big burst of flavor. Don't worry; it's much tastier than the Salisbury steaks of your youth!

MAKES 6 OVAL PATTIES

1 (15 oz [425 g]) can kidney beans drained and rinsed

½ cup (35 g) minced mushrooms

½ cup (112 g) sweet potato or pumpkin purée

¾ cup (69 g) rolled oats

2 tablespoons (14 g) ground flaxseed mixed with 4 tablespoons (59 ml) warm water

2 tablespoons (30 ml) vegan Worcestershire sauce

2 teaspoons (10 g) ground coriander

2 teaspoons (10 g) smoked paprika

1 teaspoon granulated garlic

1 teaspoon dried thyme

¾ teaspoon salt (or to taste)

½ teaspoon sage

¼ to ½ teaspoon black pepper, to taste

Preheat the oven to 350°F (177°C). Tear a piece of parchment paper to fit a small baking sheet and set both aside.

Mash the kidney beans in a medium bowl with a potato masher. There can be some chunks left. Mix in the rest of the ingredients until thoroughly combined.

Portion the mix into six oval patties on the baking sheet. The mixture will be very wet so don't try to make the patties in your hands. Instead, make 6 piles of the mixture on the parchment-lined baking sheet, press down with a spatula and then shape the edges with your hands.

Bake for 20 to 30 minutes or until the middle is firm. Serve with mashed potatoes, mushroom gravy and roasted green beans for an old-fashioned yet healthy dinner.

PER PATTY: Calories 131.2, protein 5.7 g, total fat 1.7 g, carbohydrates 23.6 g, sodium 449.2 mg, fiber 6.2 g

EGGPLANT PIZZA SLIDERS

SOY-FREE, GLUTEN-FREE, OIL-FREE OPTION*

Sometimes you're craving a decadent treat but want something healthy and guilt-free. These little sliders have a base of cooked eggplant and rolled oats flavored with sun-dried tomatoes, basil and oregano.

MAKES 26 SLIDERS

1 to 2 tablespoons (15 to 30 ml) olive oil (*water sauté instead)

1 cup (160 g) minced onion

3 cloves garlic, minced

½ cup (74 g) green pepper, minced

3 tablespoons (10 g) sun-dried tomatoes, minced

2 teaspoons (10 g) dried basil

2 teaspoons (10 g) dried oregano

¼ to ½ teaspoon red pepper flakes, optional

1 tablespoon (15 ml) tomato paste

½ teaspoon salt

1 cup (237 ml) water

5 cups (410 g) peeled and diced eggplant

1 cup (92 g) rolled oats, chopped small in food processor

1 tablespoon (6 g) nutritional yeast

Heat the oil (*or water) in a Dutch oven over medium heat. Once hot add onion and sauté until translucent, about 10 minutes. Add garlic and green pepper and sauté for another 5 minutes.

Add the sun-dried tomatoes, basil, oregano, red pepper flakes, tomato paste, salt, water and eggplant to the pot. Cover and cook over medium-low heat until the eggplant is fully cooked. The eggplant will meld into the mixture after 30 to 45 minutes.

When the eggplant is just right, remove the cover. If there is a lot of liquid, cook a little longer. Remove the pot from heat and stir in rolled oats and nutritional yeast. Cover and leave off the heat for about 15 minutes or until the oats thicken up the mixture.

Preheat the oven to 350°F (177°C) and prepare two cookie sheets with parchment paper (*or by spraying them with oil).

Using a 2½ or 3-tablespoon (37 to 45 g) scoop, portion out the sliders on the cookie sheets and flatten with the back of the scoop. Cook for 15 to 20 minutes or until they are just firm enough to flip.

They will still be soft, so flip carefully. Cook for another 15 to 20 minutes or until they seem firm. Serve on dinner or slider rolls.

PER SLIDER: Calories 35.2, protein 0.9 g, total fat 1.3 g, carbohydrates 3.8 g, sodium 23.8 mg, fiber 0.9 g

Serving Suggestion: Toast your slider rolls in the oven with marinara sauce on the bottom piece and some vegan shredded cheese on the top piece.

VEGGIE OAT TACO MINCE

GLUTEN-FREE, SOY-FREE, OIL-FREE OPTION*

Steel-cut oats mimic the mouthfeel of vegan crumbles while being completely free of processed ingredients. They also add heartiness to the veggie and bean mixture. This is the perfect way to sneak in some veggies for the picky eaters in your house. My picky eater, Cheryl, loves this!

MAKES ENOUGH FOR 8 TACOS

1 cup (237 ml) water

¼ cup (20 g) steel-cut oats

¼ cup (27.5 g) minced carrots

1 tablespoon (15 ml) olive oil (*or use water to make no oil added)

½ small onion, minced (about ¼ cup [50 g])

¼ cup (37 g) minced green pepper

2 cloves garlic, minced

1 teaspoon chili powder

1 teaspoon dried oregano

1 teaspoon cumin

1 (14 oz [500 ml]) can kidney beans, drained and rinsed

1 tablespoon (15 g) chopped green chilies

1 cup (67 g) minced kale (or other green)

juice of ½ a lime

2 tablespoons (2g) to ¼ cup (4 g) cilantro, to taste

salt, to taste

In a saucepan, bring the water, oats and carrots to a boil, then turn the heat to low. Cook for 15 to 20 minutes or until the steel-cut oats are cooked through but still chewy.

While the oats are cooking, heat the olive oil in a large sauté pan over medium heat. Add the onion and sauté until translucent, then add the green pepper, garlic and spices and cook for another 2 minutes.

Once the oat mixture is cooked, add it to the sauté pan and mix the oats in with the veggies.

You want to keep cooking until the oats dry out some and begin to separate. Keep cooking until it starts to look like crumbles.

Mix in the kidney beans, green chilies and kale. Cook until the kidney beans are thoroughly heated. Right before serving, add the lime juice, cilantro and salt. Serve in hard or soft taco shells, or in burritos. They are also amazing on top of nachos.

PER ⅛ RECIPE: Calories 87.8, protein 4.0 g, total fat 2.2 g, carbohydrates 14.6 g, sodium 108.8 mg, fiber 4.3 g

{ Feel free to leave out the beans and replace the chili powder and cumin with basil and thyme. You can also leave out the green chilies and green pepper and replace with either sliced mushrooms or sun-dried tomatoes. You can also use both to make a nice lasagna filling. }

BURGERS OF BEANY GOODNESS

GLUTEN-FREE, SOY-FREE, OIL-FREE

These simple bean burgers are not only easy to throw together on a weeknight, but they are full of flavor too. This recipe makes my favorites. We have them on buns, on top of salads and crumbled up in burritos. Make a double batch and freeze some for later.

MAKES 4 PATTIES

1 (15 oz [439 g]) can of black beans, drained and rinsed

½ cups (48 g) rolled oats

¼ cup (37 g) minced bell pepper

¼ cup (27.5 g) grated carrot

2 tablespoons (14 g) ground flaxseed mixed with 4 tablespoons (59 ml) warm water

¾ teaspoons granulated garlic

¾ teaspoons smoked paprika

½ teaspoon cumin powder

½ teaspoon oregano

¼ teaspoon onion powder

¼ teaspoon chili powder

salt and pepper, to taste

Preheat the oven to 350°F (177°C). Cover a cookie sheet with parchment paper.

Mash the black beans in a bowl with a potato masher and then add all the other ingredients except for the salt and pepper. Let the mixture sit for 10 minutes so the oats can expand a little.

Add salt and pepper to the mix. The mixture will be wet, so make 4 even piles and gently form into patties about 1" (2.5-cm) thick.

Bake 20 minutes on one side, then using a large spatula carefully flip them over and bake 10 to 15 minutes until the middle is firm.

PER PATTY: Calories 205.1, protein 11.9 g, total fat 2.5 g, carbohydrates 35.1 g, sodium 5.8 mg, fiber 11.7 g

STIR-FRIED VEGGIE OATS

GLUTEN-FREE, OIL-FREE OPTION

Oats stand in for the traditional rice in this stir-fried dish. Feel free to change up the veggies to use up what you already have in the fridge. If you use the kala namak, also known as black salt, it will add a slight eggy flavor to your dish.

MAKES 4 SERVINGS

1 cup (237 ml) water

1 cup (92 g) rolled oats

¼ cup (60 ml) low sodium soy sauce

1 tablespoon (5 g) grated ginger

1 tablespoon (14 g) toasted sesame oil or tahini

1 teaspoon yellow miso, optional

2 cloves garlic, minced

½ (15.5 oz) container of extra firm tofu (I used Trader Joe's sprouted)

½ teaspoon turmeric

½ teaspoon kala namak, optional

pinch ground black pepper

⅛ teaspoon granulated garlic

1 to 2 tablespoons (15ml to 30 ml) olive oil or veggie broth

2 cups (142 g) broccoli florets (fresh or frozen)

2 cups (364 g) frozen mixed veggies or fresh veggies cut in a small dice

1 tablespoon (15 g) black sesame seeds

1 cup (67 g) minced kale or other green

Add the water to a small saucepan and bring to a boil. Add the rolled oats and turn heat to low, cooking for 10 minutes. When they are done, remove the saucepan from heat.

Make the sauce by combining the soy sauce, ginger, sesame oil, miso (if using) and garlic in a measuring cup.

Make the scrambled tofu by crumbling the tofu and mixing in the turmeric, kala namak (if using), black pepper and granulated garlic.

Now that all the parts are ready to go, heat a large sauté pan over medium-high heat. Add the broccoli, mixed veggies and black sesame seeds. Cook for about 5 minutes, then add the cooked oats and sauce. The mixture will be fairly wet and will never dry out like rice would. Turn heat to medium and cook about 7 minutes until the veggies are almost done.

Mix in the scrambled tofu and greens and cook until the tofu is thoroughly warmed.

Serve with sriracha on the side to spice things up a bit if you want.

PER SERVING: Calories 302.9, protein 12.7 g, total fat 13.0 g, carbohydrates 32.2 g, sodium 651.5 mg, fiber 6.0 g

{ This is a one-dish meal that cooks quickly once you have all the elements prepped and ready to go. You can even do that the night before so all you have to do is throw everything in the night you want to make it. Change the veggies to use what's in season—just make sure you have a few bright colors in the mix to keep it pretty. }

TEMPEH OAT BRUSSELS SPROUT SCRAMBLE

GLUTEN-FREE, OIL-FREE OPTION*

This scramble is autumn in a bite. I love Brussels sprouts with a tang of apple cider vinegar mixed with the sweetness of maple syrup. Add in tempeh, tons of colorful vegetables and a little liquid smoke, and you'll have a dish that you'll love any time of the year.

MAKES 6 SERVINGS

1 teaspoon liquid smoke

1 (8 oz [227 g]) package tempeh, steamed and diced

2 tablespoons (30 ml) olive oil (*or broth sauté)

1 cup cooked steel-cut oats (½ cup [40 g] oats cooked with 1 cup [237 ml] water)

2 cups (176 g) shredded Brussels sprouts

1 cup (110 g) shredded carrot

½ cup (35 g) shredded red cabbage

2 tablespoons (30 ml) maple syrup

½ teaspoon liquid smoke

salt and pepper, to taste

MARINADE

1 tablespoon (20 g) maple syrup

1 tablespoon (15 ml) soy sauce

1 teaspoon apple cider vinegar

½ cup (118 ml) white wine (substitute broth or water if you don't imbibe)

½ cup (120 ml) vegetable broth (or water with 1 vegan bouillon cube)

Mix the marinade ingredients together in a container that has a tight-fitting lid. Add in the steamed tempeh, cover and marinate in fridge for 1 to 24 hours.

Heat the olive oil over medium-high heat. Once it's hot, add the cooked steel-cut oats and break up with a spatula. It's okay if there are still some clumps. Add in the tempeh, marinade, Brussels sprouts, carrot and cabbage, and sauté until the veggies are tender.

Once the liquid has mostly evaporated, add in the maple syrup and liquid smoke and mix in well. Before serving, add salt and pepper to taste.

PER SERVING: Calories 270.7, protein 12.5 g, total fat 10.4 g, carbohydrates 33.8 g, sodium 258.4 mg, fiber 4.5 g

INDIAN OATS UPMA

SOY-FREE, GLUTEN-FREE, OIL-FREE OPTION*

Oat upma is toasted rolled oats cooked with assorted veggies and spices, then topped with fresh chopped cilantro. This is not a spicy dish, but it is very flavorful from the whole spices; it makes a great dinner or a savory breakfast.

MAKES 4 SERVINGS

2 cups (184 g) rolled oats

2 tablespoons (30 ml) olive oil (*or use broth)

2 teaspoons (10 g) cumin seeds

1 teaspoon mustard seeds

1 teaspoon turmeric

½ teaspoon ground cinnamon

3 cardamom pods

10 crushed curry leaves or ½ teaspoon curry leaf powder

½ cup (80 g) minced onion

½ cup (74 g) bell pepper, minced

2 cloves garlic, minced

2 tablespoons (12 g) minced ginger

2 cups (364 g) bite-sized mixed veggies (peas, carrots, green beans, cauliflower, etc.)

2 cups (474 ml) water

salt and pepper, to taste

1 bunch fresh cilantro, chopped

Toast the oats in a large sauté pan over medium heat for 3 to 5 minutes, then set aside.

In a Dutch oven or small soup pot, heat the oil over medium heat. Once warm, sauté the cumin seeds, mustard seeds, turmeric, cinnamon and cardamom. Cook until fragrant, about 3 to 5 minutes.

Add in the curry leaves and onion and sauté until translucent, about 5 minutes, then add the bell pepper, garlic, ginger and chopped veggies. Cook for another 3 to 5 minutes until the pot becomes a little dry, then add the water and turn the heat to high.

Once the water almost comes to a boil, lower the heat to a simmer and let the veggies cook for about 10 minutes. Stir in the oats, cover and cook for 5 more minutes.

Serve topped with cilantro.

PER SERVING: Calories 285.8, protein 8.5 g, total fat 10.6 g, carbohydrates 42.6 g, sodium 44.4 mg, fiber 8.4 g

OAT DOSA

SOY-FREE, GLUTEN-FREE, OIL-FREE OPTION*

Dosas are Indian crepes, and there are many kinds of them. This recipe builds on the wheat (rava) dosa. Unlike a French crepe, this one will be crispy. The more lacey holes that you get in your dosa, the crispier it will be. To make these, do the exact opposite of what you would do to make a French crepe.

MAKES ABOUT 6 SMALL DOSAS

½ cup (48 g) rolled oats, processed to a powder, it does not have to be as fine as flour, just a coarse grind

¼ cup (40 g) rice flour

¼ cup (32 g) semolina flour

¼ cup (4 g) chopped cilantro

1 teaspoon cumin seeds

1 teaspoon torn curry leaves (dried or fresh), optional

⅛ teaspoon chili powder

pinch salt

pinch black pepper

1½ to 2 cups (355 to 474 ml) water

Mix the oats, flours, cilantro, cumin, curry leaves, chili powder, salt and pepper together in a bowl. Add in 1½ cups (355 ml) of the water and stir well. Let sit for 10 minutes.

The batter should be pretty watery, but you may need to add more water as you go along.

Heat a griddle or pancake pan (flat bottom) over medium heat. You can spray a little oil before cooking each dosa or use a nonstick pan and wipe out between dosas.

With a ¼ cup measuring scoop, lightly pour the batter in a circle on the hot pan. Start with the outside outline and then pour inside of that. Cook on one side until the edges begin to look dry (about 2 to 3 minutes) then flip and cook 1 to 2 minutes more. (You may need more time if yours doesn't have many holes.)

Repeat until you've used all your batter. Serve with coconut chutney (recipe below).

PER DOSA: Calories 74.1, protein 2.1 g, total fat 0.7 g, carbohydrates 14.9 g, sodium 25.8 mg, fiber 1.2 g

> Hing or Asafoetida is used in Indian cooking to enhance the flavor. It has a very strong smell and needs to be stored away from other spices.

EASY COCONUT CHUTNEY

SOY-FREE, OIL-FREE, GLUTEN-FREE
MAKES ABOUT ½ CUP (120 G)

½ teaspoon crushed curry leaves (dried or fresh), optional

¼ teaspoon cumin seeds

¼ teaspoon mustard seeds

pinch chili powder

pinch hing, optional

¼ to ½ cup (60ml to 120 ml) water

½ cup (40 g) finely shredded coconut

2 teaspoons (10 g) grated ginger

Mix all the ingredients together in a small bowl. You can dip your dosa in or spread it on top.

> I tried making these dosas with rolled oats, but it would work just as well and be chewier with steel-cut oats. Just cook them per package directions, since they need to cook much longer than the rolled oats.

APPLE–THYME SAVORY STEEL-CUT OATS WITH SEARED VEGAN SAUSAGE

OIL-FREE

The apple adds a hint of sweetness to this oatmeal, but it definitely gets its savory taste from the herbs. You could eat it plain; I love having the seared vegan sausage coins on top. You could also roast a can of drained and rinsed chickpeas with the spices from 1 recipe of Steel-Cut Oat Sausage Crumbles (recipe on page 26). This would make it gluten-free and soy-free in addition to oil-free!

MAKES 2 SERVINGS

1½ cups (355 ml) water

½ cup (80 g) steel-cut oats

1 medium apple, peeled and chopped small

½ teaspoon thyme

⅛ teaspoon ground rosemary

⅛ teaspoon garlic powder

salt and pepper, to taste

2 vegan Italian sausages cut into coins and seared

Add the water, oats and apples to a small saucepan and bring to a boil. Turn to medium-low, and add thyme, rosemary and garlic powder. Cook for 15 to 20 minutes or until the oats are tender. Make sure to stir every 5 to 10 minutes so the oats don't get stuck to the bottom.

While the oats are cooking, heat a nonstick skillet over medium heat, and cook the vegan sausage coins until they brown on one side. Then flip and brown on the other side.

When the oats are done, stir in salt and pepper to taste. Serve topped with the crispy vegan sausage coins.

PER SERVING: Calories 487.5, protein 36.3 g, total fat 16.2 g, carbohydrates 53.6 g, sodium 621.0 mg, fiber 15.2 g

MUSHROOM SUN-DRIED TOMATO STEEL-CUT OAT RISOTTO

GLUTEN-FREE, SOY-FREE, OIL-FREE OPTION*

There's more than one way to get your daily dose of oats! This mushroom risotto has the perfect al dente texture and has a B-vitamin boost from the nutritional yeast. You'll be surprised at how well the steel-cut oats mimic that chewiness normally provided by Arborio rice. Plus, oats are much cheaper!

MAKES 4 SERVINGS

1 to 2 tablespoons (15 to 30 ml) olive oil (*or use water to make oil-free)

½ small onion, minced

2 cloves of garlic, minced

1½ cups (105 g) minced mushrooms

¼ cup (37 g) minced green bell pepper

1 teaspoon dried basil

1 teaspoon dried oregano

½ teaspoon dried marjoram

⅛ teaspoon ground rosemary or ¼ teaspoon regular rosemary

1 cup (80 g) steel-cut oats

2 tablespoons (7 g) minced sun-dried tomatoes

4 to 5 cups (946 to 1183 ml) water or vegetable broth

2 tablespoons (12 g) nutritional yeast

salt and pepper, to taste

Heat the olive oil over medium heat in a saucepan or Dutch oven with a thick bottom until it sizzles when you add a tiny drop of water to the pan.

Add onions and cook until translucent, then add the garlic, mushrooms, bell pepper and herbs. Sauté the veggies for 5 to 20 minutes, until the mushrooms have browned and released their juices.

Add in the oats, and stir to prevent them from burning. Cook until lightly toasted, about 3 minutes. Add the sun-dried tomatoes and 1 cup (237 ml) of water. Simmer over medium heat, stirring often to keep the mixture from burning on the bottom.

Once the first cup of water has been absorbed by the oats, add a second cup of water and keep stirring. Add the third cup of water once the second is absorbed and keep stirring (isn't risotto fun?). When the third cup is absorbed, add one more cup water (the fourth). After it's absorbed, try a bite of the oats to see if it's cooked through. You want it to be al dente, still tender but a little chewy.

If it's not tender yet, add an additional cup of water. The oats should still have a chewy texture and not be mushy. Right before serving, add the nutritional yeast, salt and pepper.

PER SERVING: Calories 135.4, protein 5.2 g, total fat 7.9 g, carbohydrates 12.8 g, sodium 39.5 mg, fiber 2.9 g

POTATO GNOCCHI

This recipe elevates oats to a new level. Your family will have no idea that there are oats in these pillowy dumplings. Don't be nervous if you haven't made gnocchi before; it's an easy and forgiving process. Gnocchi are traditionally made with semolina flour and potatoes. We're using oat flour in place of wheat, which makes these little dumplings gluten-free.

MAKES ABOUT 6 DOZEN

4 russet potatoes

1½ cups (150 g) oat flour (or finely ground rolled oats)

½ teaspoon salt

Peel the potatoes and cut into small chunks. Boil until tender, and drain well in a colander. Transfer to a large mixing bowl and mash well.

Add in ½ cup (50 g) of the flour and salt. Mix well with your hands, adding the other 1 cup (100 g) of flour a ½ cup (50 g) at a time.

Flour a large cutting board and turn out the dough. Cut into 8 equal portions, then roll each one out into a thin snake (about ½-inch [1.3-cm] thick). Cut into small ¾-inch (1.9-cm) thick pieces.

You can leave them as is or press them against a fork to press the lines in the gnocchi for the classic "line" look.

Boil the gnocchi about 2 dozen at a time in a large pot of water until they float to the top, about 2 to 4 minutes.

PER 12 GNOCCHI: Calories 156.7, protein 5.7 g, total fat 2.3 g, carbohydrates 33.1 g, sodium 186.7 mg, fiber 4.3 g

CAJUN-STUFFED BELL PEPPERS

GLUTEN-FREE, SOY-FREE, OIL-FREE

You've heard that having some cooked grain ready in the fridge always makes your life easier. Most of us forget that cooked steel-cut oats can be used like most other grains; the proof is in the stuffed peppers!

MAKES 4 SERVINGS

4 large bell peppers

1 cup (234 g) cooked steel-cut oats

1 (15oz [425 g]) can of black-eyed peas or kidney beans

¼ cup (59 ml) vegetable broth

1 tablespoon plus 1 teaspoon (20 ml) tomato paste

1 teaspoon marjoram

1 teaspoon thyme

1 teaspoon Cajun spice blend

¼ teaspoon granulated garlic

½ teaspoon salt

¼ teaspoon black pepper

Preheat the oven to 350°F (177°C), and either oil or put parchment paper on the bottom of a casserole pan.

Cut the tops off the 4 bell peppers, remove the seeds and trim away the white from the ribs. Set aside.

In a mixing bowl, combine the oats, black-eyed peas, broth, tomato paste, herbs, spices, garlic, salt and pepper. Mix well and stuff into the bell peppers. Place the filled bell peppers in the casserole dish, cover with foil and bake 40 minutes.

PER SERVING: Calories 339.7, protein 13.1 g, total fat 4.8 g, carbohydrates 62.0 g, sodium 612.4 mg, fiber 12.1 g

{ Top with some shredded vegan cheese after 30 minutes of baking and bake uncovered for the last 10. }

INDIAN-SPICED LEMON OATS

GLUTEN-FREE, SOY-FREE, OIL-FREE OPTION

This is a savory oat dish that combines the tartness of lemon juice with the richness of cashews. It has a few unusual ingredients, but I've listed easy-to-find alternatives. The two Indian lentils are soaked and create a crunch like minced peanuts, so if you don't have them, you can just use peanuts in their place.

MAKES 2 SERVINGS

2 tablespoons (30 g) chana dal (or peanuts)

2 teaspoons (10 g) urad dal (or peanuts)

2 teaspoons (10 ml) olive oil (or use water or broth)

½ teaspoon mustard seeds

¼ teaspoon cumin seeds

¼ teaspoon coriander seeds

pinch chili powder

2 teaspoons (10 g) grated ginger

2 tablespoons (30 g) cashews

½ cup (48 g) rolled oats

5 curry leaves, optional

1 cup (237 ml) water

juice of ½ a lemon

salt, to taste

Put the chana dal and urad dal in a small bowl and cover with water. Let soak for 25 minutes to soften.

Heat the oil in a large sauté pan over medium-high heat. Once hot, add the mustard seeds, cumin seeds, coriander seeds and chili powder and sauté about 3 to 5 minutes until fragrant. Then add the ginger, cashews, oats and optional curry leaves. Cook about 5 minutes until the oats are lightly toasted.

Add the water and turn the heat to high until it begins to boil. Lower heat to medium and stir until the water is absorbed and begins to dry slightly. Add lemon juice and salt to taste before serving.

PER SERVING: Calories 260.3, protein 9.8 g, total fat 10.9 g, carbohydrates 33.3 g, sodium 23.9 mg, fiber 4.0 g

SUNFLOWER SEED AND BEAN OAT–LOAF

Everyone needs at least one healthy no-meat loaf recipe up their sleeves. This one is made up of cannellini beans, sunflower seeds, herbs and, of course, oats. Don't let the long list of ingredients fool you, because this is a snap to make.

MAKES 8 SERVINGS

1½ cups (140 g) rolled oats

1 cup (135 g) roasted sunflower seeds

2 (15 oz [420 g]) cans cannellini beans or 3 cups homemade

4 tablespoons (28 g) ground flaxseed mixed with 8 tablespoons (118 ml) warm water

2 tablespoons (33 g) tomato paste

2 cloves garlic, minced

3 tablespoons (18 g) nutritional yeast

1½ teaspoons (1 g) basil

1 teaspoon marjoram

1 teaspoon thyme

1 teaspoon vegan Worcestershire sauce

½ teaspoon rubbed sage

½ teaspoon ground black pepper

½ teaspoon salt

¼ teaspoon ground rosemary

TOPPING INGREDIENTS
½ cup (120 g) ketchup

1 tablespoon (17 ml) vegan Worcestershire sauce

Preheat the oven to 350°F (177°C) and oil a loaf pan.

Mix the oats and sunflower seeds in a mixing bowl and set aside.

In a food processor, combine the cannellini beans, flaxseed mixture, tomato paste, garlic, nutritional yeast, basil, marjoram, thyme, vegan Worcestershire sauce, rubbed sage, ground black pepper, salt and ground rosemary. Process until smooth, then scrape out into the dry mixture of oats and sunflower seeds.

Mix until well combined, and put the mixture into the oiled loaf pan.

In a small bowl, mix the topping ingredients and spread over the top of the loaf. Cover with foil and bake for 45 minutes. Take off the foil and bake for 15 minutes more.

Serve with mashed potatoes and steamed veggies.

PER SERVING: Calories 277.1, protein 13.0 g, total fat 11.8 g, carbohydrates 32.1 g, sodium 209.0 mg, fiber 4.4 g

CAULIFLOWER OAT PIZZA CRUST

GLUTEN-FREE, SOY-FREE, OIL-FREE

One innovation that the Paleo food movement has brought to the table is all the wonderful things made from cauliflower. Here's a pizza crust with cauliflower as the main ingredient. While this crust isn't grain-free, it is gluten-free and lower calorie.

MAKES 1 THIN PIZZA CRUST (6 SERVINGS)

1 cup (92 g) rolled oats

½ medium head cauliflower

¼ cup (28 g) ground flaxseed mixed with ½ cup (120 ml) warm water

1 teaspoon dried basil

¼ teaspoon ground rosemary

¼ teaspoon salt

Preheat oven to 400°F (204°C). Line a large cookie sheet with parchment paper and set aside. Process the oats into a flour (or as close to flour as you can) in your food processor, then pour into a large mixing bowl.

Process cauliflower in your food processor until it looks like tiny grains of couscous or millet. Then pour 3 cups of the cauliflower into the large mixing bowl with the oats. You can use any leftovers in stews, soup or rice or even sauté a small batch as faux rice for another dinner.

Mix the rest of the ingredients together and pat into a rectangle on the cookie sheet. Make this as thin as possible to create a crunchy crust that holds together well.

Bake for 25 to 30 minutes or until the edges turn brown and the crust has cooked at least half way through.

Pull the crust out and add sauce, veggies and vegan cheese. Bake another 10 to 15 minutes. The crust will not get crunchy in the middle, so be prepared to eat this pizza with a fork.

PER PIZZA CRUST: Calories 123, protein 5.7 g, total fat 3.9 g, carbohydrates 19 g, sodium 0 mg, fiber 5.9 g

NO-KNEAD MULTIGRAIN PIZZA CRUST

SOY-FREE, OIL-FREE, GLUTEN-FREE OPTION*

Here's a no-guilt pizza dough that's full of whole wheat and spelt along with oats, of course. Mix up the dough for the crust before work, and it will be ready to go when you get home. Cooking from Julie Hasson's *Vegan Pizza* gave me the inspiration to branch off to create my own oaty version.

MAKES 2 THIN PIZZA CRUSTS

1 cup (237 ml) warm water

1 teaspoon agave nectar, maple syrup or sugar

2 teaspoons (10 g) yeast, room temperature

1 cup (120 g) white whole wheat flour or regular whole wheat flour (*use gluten-free baking mix)

1 cup (120 g) spelt flour (or use more whole wheat flour)

1 cup (224 g) oat flour (or 1 cup [225 g] rolled oats processed fine)

1 teaspoon salt

Preheat oven to 425°F (218°C) and either oil a pizza pan or use a nonstick one.

Measure out 1 cup (235 ml) of warm—not hot—water. It should feel warm to the touch but not hot to the inside of your wrist. If it is too hot, it will kill the yeast.

Stir the agave nectar into the water and sprinkle the yeast on top. Let sit for 5 to 10 minutes. The yeast should grow in size, indicating that it's ready to go.

Mix the flours and salt together in a large mixing bowl. When the yeast mixture is ready, add it to the flours and mix well.

Cover the dough and put in a warm, draft-free place for 3 to 4 hours. The dough will grow larger—but may not double—especially if it's a cold day. Please note that you can leave the dough for longer while you are away from work so that it can rise.

Flour a large cutting board (with any of the flours you are using) and either roll out half the dough into a thin round pizza or use all the dough and make a thick one.

Top with a red sauce, pesto, veggies and even nondairy cheese—really whatever you'd normally like on your pizza.

Depending on how thick the crust is, bake for 10 to 15 minutes.

PER PIZZA CRUST: Calories 345.5, protein 11.1 g, total fat 3.8 g, carbohydrates 66.1 g, sodium 0.3 mg, fiber 10.5 g

{ I use a nonstick pizza pan that has holes in the bottom of it. This makes a crispy thin-crust pizza. You can use a pizza stone, a regular pizza pan or even a cast iron skillet if that's what you prefer. }

CHAPTER SEVEN

DELIGHTFUL DESSERTS

Remember warm cookies fresh from the oven after school or an apple crumb dessert served after dinner? Oats seep into our memories and always find their way into happy everyday events.

I admit that when I had the idea for this book I wasn't thinking of having a dessert chapter at all. However, my testers talked me into it and, as usual, they were right. I think you will enjoy these oat-inspired goodies, too.

I have a few oatmeal cookies: an old-fashioned recipe that has you pick your own mix-ins, so you can re-create the cookies from your childhood; a coconut variation, with just a hint of almond; and finally a crunchy oat shortbread that's flavored with bourbon.

I've dressed up the obligatory crumble in its holiday finery to create a gingerbread pear crumble and decked out a pie with an oatmeal cookie crust. I'm sharing Ann Oliverio's delicious Humble Pie, a chai-spiced oatmeal tart that I know you're going to love.

For a change of pace, I have mini fat-free raspberry cakes that are super moist from vegan yogurt. (Make sure to look in the chapter on Do It Yourself Homemade Staples, which begins on page 17, to learn how to make your own oat milk yogurt at home.)

Little healthy turtle truffle bites come together quickly and make a great gift. The chocolate terrine is made by cooking a thick oat groat milk until it becomes pudding-like and then cooling it in the refrigerator until it magically firms up enough to slice.

GINGERBREAD PEAR CRUMBLE

SOY-FREE, GLUTEN-FREE OPTION*, OIL-FREE OPTION**

This is a wonderful way to keep your holidays healthy, and it takes less time to make than a batch of cookies. If you aren't a huge molasses fan, you can use half the amount or even replace it with another sweetener. Depending on what you have on hand, use either apples or a combination of pears and apples.

MAKES 8 SERVINGS

TOPPING INGREDIENTS

1 cup (96 g) rolled oats

1 cup (132 g) whole wheat pastry flour (*use a gluten-free baking mix)

¼ cup (60 ml) agave nectar

2 tablespoons (40 g) molasses

1½ teaspoons ground ginger

1 teaspoon cinnamon

¼ teaspoon allspice

¼ teaspoon nutmeg

⅛ teaspoon cloves

FILLING INGREDIENTS

5 cups (805 g) chopped pears (peeled if not organic)

2 tablespoons (30 ml) agave nectar, optional

pinch of salt

Preheat the oven to 350°F (177°C). Spray a 2-quart casserole dish with oil. (**You can also line with parchment paper or use a nonstick pan to make it oil-free.)

Combine all of the topping ingredients together in a bowl and mix well. Set aside.

If your pears aren't very sweet, add 2 tablespoons (30 ml) of agave nectar and a pinch of salt.

Spread out the pear mixture in the casserole dish.

Crumble the gingerbread topping over the pears, then bake for 30 minutes.

PER SERVING: Calories 202.3, protein 3.1 g, total fat 1.1 g, carbohydrates 47.2 g, sodium 1.9 mg, fiber 5.7 g

{ Serve this in the summer by using berries or stone fruit as your star ingredient or replacing the molasses with agave nectar or the sweetener of your choice to taste. Leave out the warming winter spices, and mix in some fresh chopped herbs like basil, thyme or mint with the fruit. }

OATMEAL COOKIE CRUSTED APPLE CRUMB PIE

GLUTEN-FREE, SOY-FREE

This pie has a homey oatmeal cookie crust and is filled with juicy spiced apples. Topped with a pecan crumb, this pie is dressed up in a tart pan, making it appropriate for both a fancy dinner party and a simple weeknight meal. Please note that you need to use a tart pan or springform pan for this to come out in one beautiful piece. If you don't have one, the pie tastes just as great served as a crumble!

MAKES 8 SERVINGS

CRUST

2 cups (193 g) rolled oats

¼ cup (52 ml) coconut oil

¼ cup (58 ml) nondairy milk

2 tablespoons (14 g) ground flaxseed mixed with 4 tablespoons warm water

2 tablespoons (30 g) coconut sugar or brown sugar

½ teaspoon cinnamon

pinch salt

FILLING

3 cups (375 g) peeled and chopped apples

1 tablespoon (15 ml) lemon juice

3 tablespoons (45 g) coconut sugar or brown sugar

1½ teaspoons cinnamon

½ teaspoon allspice

⅛ teaspoon ground cloves

TOPPING

¼ cup (28 g) pecans

Preheat the oven to 350°F (177°C) and spray an 8" (20-cm) tart or springform pan with oil. Set aside for later. (Please note that if you do not use a pan with a removable bottom, the bottom pie crust will crumble.)

Toast the oats in a dry nonstick sauté pan on medium heat. Keep stirring so they do not burn. The oats are done when fragrant. It will take about 3 to 5 minutes.

Add all the crust ingredients into a food processor and pulse until it starts to come together and form a ball. You may need to stop and scrape down the bowl a few times before pulsing again. Take about ⅔ of the mix out of the food processor, leaving ⅓ for the topping, and press into the tart pan with your hands to form the crust.

Mix all the filling ingredients together in a mixing bowl, then pour into the prepared crust.

You will now finish making the topping. ⅓ of the crust ingredients should still be in the food processor, so throw in the pecans and process until the pecans are tiny. Crumble this over the top of the pie and bake for 30 to 40 minutes, until the crust sets up and the top browns.

Cool completely before you try to remove the pie from the tart pan and serve.

PER SERVING: Calories 215.5, protein 3.3 g, total fat 11.7 g, carbohydrates 22.2 g, sodium 7.9 mg, fiber 2.9 g

HUMBLE PIE:

ANN'S CHAI-SPICED OATMEAL TART WITH WARM COCONUT-VANILLA SAUCE

GLUTEN-FREE, SOY-FREE, OIL-FREE

I have to try every vegan chai-inspired recipe that I come across. This one has a date-walnut crust that holds the oatmeal chai filling with raspberries. This recipe is the work of one of my favorite vegan bloggers, Ann Oliverio of AnUnrefinedVegan.com. Her recipes are always fun and innovative, like this elevated twist to an old-fashioned oatmeal pie. Thanks, Ann!

MAKES 8 SERVINGS

CRUST

1½ cups (227 g) figs chopped with stems removed

1 cup (110 g) walnuts

4 dates, chopped

¼ cup (35 g) crystallized ginger

dash of cinnamon and ground cardamom

2 tablespoons (30 ml) water

1 cup (123 g) fresh or thawed frozen raspberries (plus more for garnish)

¼ cup (80 g) fruit-juice sweetened raspberry preserves

MAKE THE CRUST

In a food processor, add the figs, walnuts and dates and process until chunky. Add the ginger, cinnamon and water and process until fairly smooth. Pat mixture into a 10" (25.4-cm) tart pan that has a removable bottom about 1½ inches (3.8-cm) deep (with removable bottom), bringing it up along the sides.

In a small bowl, lightly crush the fresh raspberries and then stir in the raspberry preserves.

Pour the mixture onto the crust and spread evenly. Cover and chill until needed.

Ann also runs the well-known Virtual Vegan Potluck twice a year. Be sure to bookmark VirtualVeganPotluck.com for recipes shared by hundreds of bloggers, or share one yourself!

FILLING

1 cup (80 g) uncooked steel-cut oats

4 cups (940 ml) strongly brewed chai tea (1 teabag per cup of water)

⅛ cup (24 g) chia seeds

1 teaspoon cinnamon

½ teaspoon ground cardamom

⅛ teaspoon ground cloves

dash black pepper

¼ teaspoon ground ginger

½ a medium orange, zested

¼ cup (38 g) dates, chopped and soaked for a few hours, then drained

3 tablespoons (45 ml) pure maple syrup

¼ cup + 1 tablespoon (75 ml) nondairy milk

1 teaspoon vanilla extract

COCONUT-VANILLA SAUCE

1 cup (225 ml) full-fat coconut milk

¼ cup (63 ml) water

½ teaspoon vanilla extract

1 teaspoon agave nectar or maple syrup

MAKE THE OATMEAL

In a medium-sized saucepan, combine the steel-cut oats with 3 cups (700 ml) of the chai tea. Cover and let sit at room temperature overnight, or for about 8 hours.

In the morning, add more tea to the oats if necessary. Bring to a boil, then turn the heat to low and simmer gently, adding more tea if the mixture becomes too dry. Stir in the chia seeds, spices and orange zest. Cook until the oats are very soft, about 20 to 25 minutes.

Meanwhile, in the bowl of a food processor, process the dates, maple syrup, milk and vanilla until smooth. Pour in about half of the oat mixture and process until smooth. Pour the processed oats back in with the whole oats and stir well.

Pour the oat mixture into the prepared crust, smooth the top and add some more raspberries if you like. Put the pie into the refrigerator to set. This only takes a couple of hours.

MAKE THE SAUCE

Combine and heat all of the sauce ingredients in a small saucepan. Keep sauce warm until you are ready to serve with the pie.

To serve, slice the pie (a wet knife helps) and warm for a few seconds in the microwave.

Drizzle with the warm sauce and sprinkle with additional raspberries.

PER SERVING: Calories 422.7, protein 7.6 g, total fat 18.1 g, carbohydrates 58.5 g, sodium 28.9 mg, fiber 6.9 g

BOURBON OAT SHORTBREAD

SOY-FREE

There's nothing quite like a bite of shortbread. It's a dense cookie that's traditionally made with flour, butter and salt, but even a few of the old recipes include oats for a nice crumbly texture. Oats are a staple in Scotland, and the small amount of bourbon gives this recipe a faint butterscotch flavor. If you don't imbibe, you could use plain vanilla extract in its place.

MAKES 12 SERVINGS

⅓ cup (70 ml) coconut oil, room temperature

⅓ cup (80 ml) vegan margarine (like Earth Balance)

⅓ cup (80 g) coconut sugar (or brown sugar)

1 tablespoon (15 ml) bourbon

⅔ cup (60 g) oat flour (or rolled oats processed into flour)

⅔ cup (80 g) whole wheat pastry flour

¼ teaspoon salt

Preheat oven to 350°F (177°C). Prepare a large cookie sheet with spray oil or by lining with parchment paper.

Cream the coconut oil, vegan margarine, coconut sugar and bourbon in a mixer or with two forks in a medium mixing bowl.

In a smaller bowl mix the flours and salt. Then add the flour mixure to the coconut oil mixture and stir until thoroughly combined.

You have a few choices on how to shape the dough: You could bake it as one big circle or rectangle. Either way, score the cookies a little more than halfway through into the size you'd like. You can also decorate the cookie segments with holes by using a fork.

Bake for 20 to 25 minutes or until the edges turn brown.

PER COOKIE: Calories 156.8, protein 1.3 g, total fat 13.2 g, carbohydrates 10.6 g, sodium 61.5 mg, fiber 1.4 g

You can also make individual cookies by using wax paper to roll the cookie dough into a log shape. Chill in the refrigerator for at least an hour and cut into slices. You can make these as thick or as thin as you want them. Bake for 8 to 10 minutes or until the edges are golden brown.

OLD-FASHIONED MIX AND MATCH OATMEAL COOKIES

SOY-FREE, GLUTEN-FREE OPTION*, OIL-FREE OPTION**

If you need something that reminds you of your childhood and puts the cheer back into your day, then this recipe is for you. These cookies are easy to make, and the best part is that you can add your favorites into the mix.

MAKES ABOUT 48 SMALLER COOKIES OR 24 LARGER ONES

OAT MIXTURE
1 cup (96 g) rolled oats
2 tablespoons (14 g) ground flaxseed
1 cup (237 ml) nondairy milk

DRY INGREDIENTS
1¼ cups (165 g) whole wheat pastry flour (*use a gluten-free baking mix)
1 teaspoon baking powder
½ teaspoon baking soda
¼ teaspoon salt

WET MIXTURE
⅓ cup (70 ml) coconut oil (**use applesauce or mashed banana to make oil-free)
⅓ cup (80 g) coconut sugar or brown sugar
¼ cup (81 ml) agave nectar or maple syrup
1 teaspoon vanilla extract

MIX-IN CHOICES (PICK 2)
½ cup (85 g) vegan chocolate chips
½ cup (70 g) chopped nuts
½ cup (75 g) chopped dried figs
½ cup (75 g) chopped dried apricots
½ cup (70 g) raisins
½ cup (60 g) dried cranberries

Preheat oven to 350°F (177°C). Spread two cookie sheets with parchment paper or spray with oil.

Combine the oat mixture ingredients in a small bowl, then set aside. Mix the dry ingredients in a separate bowl.

Cream the coconut oil and coconut sugar together in a mixer or with 2 forks in a large bowl. Once it comes together and is fluffy, mix in the agave nectar and vanilla. Then add the oat mixture and mix well.

Add half the dry mixture and mix until just incorporated, then add the other half with your mix-ins and thoroughly combine.

Use a 1-tablespoon (15-g) cookie scoop to make the cookies and press flat with the back of a spoon or your hand. Bake for about 15 minutes or until the cookies are slightly brown on top and caramel brown underneath.

Repeat until all the cookies are baked, and store in an airtight container. If you don't want that many cookies all at once, you can freeze some of the measured-out cookie dough in parchment paper and surprise your family with warm cookies fresh out of the oven another time with almost no effort!

PER LARGE COOKIE (WITH CHOCOLATE CHIPS AND NUTS): Calories 56.4, protein 1.0 g, total fat 2.8 g, carbohydrates 7.4 g, sodium 28.0 mg, fiber 0.8 g

- If you'd like to lower the sugar content but keep all the sweetness, use ¼ teaspoon of stevia plus ¼ cup (80 ml) milk in place of the agave.
- Add ½ to 1 teaspoon of your favorite ground spice like cinnamon, nutmeg or cardamom to spice things up.
- Try white chocolate with fresh cranberries for a holiday treat.

MINI RASPBERRY CAKES

SOY-FREE, OIL-FREE, GLUTEN-FREE OPTION*

These perfectly portioned and moist fat-free cakes are an easy end to a relaxing dinner at home. You could drizzle some chocolate over the top, like Guilt-free Stevia Chocolate Syrup (page 33), but I personally love them just as they are. Freeze a few leftovers in single servings to have whenever you crave something sweet.

MAKES 18 MINI CAKES

DRY INGREDIENTS

2 cups (180 g) oat flour (or make your own from rolled oats page 13)

1 cup (132 g) whole wheat pastry flour (*use gluten-free baking mix)

1 cup (150 g) almond flour

1 tablespoon (15 g) baking powder

½ teaspoon baking soda

¼ teaspoon salt

WET INGREDIENTS

1 cup (227 g) plain vegan yogurt

½ cup (100 g) coconut sugar or brown sugar

¼ cup (60 g) agave nectar

2 tablespoons (14 g) ground flaxseeds mixed with 4 tablespoons warm water

2 teaspoons (10 ml) vanilla

1 (120 oz [340 g]) bag of frozen raspberries

Preheat your oven to 350°F (177°C), and either line the muffin tins with paper liners to keep the recipe oil-free or spray with oil to prepare.

Mix all the dry ingredients in a small bowl. In a larger bowl, mix all the wet ingredients except the raspberries.

Add the dry to the wet, mix well and then fold in the raspberries. Portion into muffin tins and bake for 25 to 30 minutes, or until the center can be touched without leaving a depression.

PER MINI CAKE: Calories 159.7, protein 4.1 g, total fat 4.5 g, carbohydrates 29.5 g, sodium 40.0 mg, fiber 3.5 g

TURTLE OAT TRUFFLES

GLUTEN-FREE, SOY-FREE, OIL-FREE

This two-bite dessert is rich with date caramel, pecans and chocolate chips all held together with oatmeal. You could leave out the chocolate chips or substitute with cocoa nibs to make this healthy enough for a morning energy bite. Resist the urge to roll these in powdered sugar, because these beauties will just soak it all in and the sugar will disappear.

MAKES 2 DOZEN TRUFFLES

1¼ cups (120 g) rolled oats

Thick Date Caramel Sauce (see recipe below)

1 cup (100 g) minced pecans

⅓ cup (57 g) vegan mini chocolate chips or chopped regular sized chips

¼ cup (20 g) finely shredded coconut or cocoa powder

Put the oats in a food processor and process until most of the oats are broken up (but not so much that it turns into oat flour). Pour into a mixing bowl.

Add the pecans, chocolate chips and the thick date caramel sauce to the oats and mix well.

Chill mixture in fridge for at least 1 hour to make it firmer and easier to roll. You can chill these overnight if that's better for your schedule.

Make truffles uniform by measuring the dough out with a 1 tablespoon (15 g) cookie scoop.

Roll each truffle into a ball with your hand, then roll in either coconut or cocoa powder. Store in the refrigerator.

PER TRUFFLE: Calories 65.2, protein 1.2 g, total fat 4.9 g, carbohydrates 5.3 g, sodium 0.2 mg, fiber 1.1 g

THICK DATE CARAMEL SAUCE

MAKES ABOUT ¾ CUP (177 ML)

15 dates

½ cup (116 ml) nondairy milk

1 teaspoon vanilla

To make the sauce, add all the ingredients to a high-speed blender* and blend until smooth. You will need to scrape down a few times during the blending process.

*If you don't have a high-speed blender, soak the dates overnight before making the caramel. This will make them softer and easier to blend.

CHOCOLATE ORANGE PUDDING

No one will guess that the main ingredient in this dazzling dessert is oats! This pudding was a last-minute inspiration. I was experimenting with oats' wonderful natural thickening ability and thought it would make the perfect texture for a rich chocolate dessert. Sometimes being a mad scientist in the kitchen pays off!

MAKES 8 SERVINGS

½ cup (80 g) oat groats, soaked at least 8 hours (or use steel-cut and soak 20 minutes)

4 cups (946 ml) water

¼ cup (21 g) cocoa powder

¼ cup (60 ml) agave nectar

¾ teaspoons stevia

½ teaspoon orange oil or 1 teaspoon orange extract

pinch salt

Blend the oats and water together, then strain in a bowl with a pour spout. Strain into a pot with a thick bottom like a Dutch oven. Whisk in the cocoa, agave nectar, stevia and salt. Heat over medium heat, whisking the whole time until the milk thickens.

Store in a covered container and refrigerate until solid.

PER SERVING: Calories 63, protein 2.3 g, total fat 1.0 g, carbohydrates 16.1 g, sodium 0.5 mg, fiber 2.4 g

{ Not a fan of orange? Use the extract of your choice like mint, lemon or even almond. }

DREAMY DARK CHOCOLATE OAT CREAM

When I was working on this book, I saw a Facebook post from a friend, Kristina Sloggett, with a luscious photo of a creamy chocolate ice cream cone. It read, "You'll never guess what this is made of!" Of course I said, "oats" and raced over to her blog, SpaBettie.com, to read her post. I thought I was probably wrong, but she actually did create this decadent yet healthy recipe with all the goodness of oats. In her words, it's the "dreamiest, creamiest, mousse-iest" vegan ice cream she ever had, and I have to agree. Luckily, Kristina is letting me share her wonderful recipe with you! Note that this recipe requires an ice cream maker.

MAKES ABOUT 6 SERVINGS (3 CUPS [709 GRAMS])

1 cup (80 g) gluten-free steel-cut oats

4 cups (945 ml) water, divided

3 Medjool dates, pitted

8 oz 72% dark chocolate
(*some dark chocolates use soy as an emulsifier—check ingredient list)

Soak oats in water overnight. Strain and rinse completely; the oats should be soft.

In a high-speed blender, combine oats, dates and 2 cups (475 ml) of water. Gradually reach the highest speed and blend until smooth. Push the mixture through a mesh strainer and return the remainder from the strainer back to the blender. Blend on high until the mixture is completely smooth. Add the strained liquid back in and blend. Set aside.

Finely chop the chocolate and add the pieces to a small saucepan. Heat chocolate on low heat, continuously stirring until completely melted. Remove the saucepan from heat, allowing it to cool slightly but not solidify.

Turn blender on low and slowly add the cooled chocolate. Once chocolate is added, blend on high. Allow the mixture to cool before adding it to the ice cream maker. Proceed using ice cream machine instructions, about 18 minutes.

The ice cream will be of soft-serve consistency and will take several hours to set in the freezer.

PER SERVING: Calories 178.3, protein 5.5 g, total fat 5.2 g, carbohydrates 28.2 g, sodium 6.7 mg, fiber 4.7 g

CHAPTER EIGHT

DRINKS, OAT MILK AND EVEN AN OAT LIQUOR

The first time I had oat milk, I was doing a milk tasting. I had at least a dozen kinds of nondairy milks, but the oat milk surprised me the most. It was thick, sweet and very creamy. Now that I've been making oat milk at home, it's been great for my grocery budget.

You can make these drinks with rolled oats, steel-cut oat or even oat groats. Oat groats take a little planning because you will need to soak them overnight before blending. Steel-cut oats need to soak for about 30 minutes before blending; rolled oats need to soak for 10 minutes. Rolled oats are almost instant, since from start to finish they take you about 15 minutes.

Save the pulp for people or puppy cookies; there's no reason to waste any of the oat goodness!

You may have a huge range of pulp left over from the blending process. I usually have ½ to 1 cup, while a few of my testers had almost none. This has to do with a number of factors, but blending a long time in a high-speed blender will result in less pulp to strain out. This may sound better and easier, but it also increases the amount of calories. The nutritional information that appears in this book factor in all the pulp, so you are looking at the highest counts. To get an exact count, you'd have to get a food scientist to test each batch you make.

We all know that making our own nondairy milk means no wasteful packaging to throw into a landfill, but oat milk costs less than almost any other nondairy milk that you can make at home. You can make 4 cups with as little as ½ cup of oats, so it is much cheaper than paying 2 to 4 dollars for a carton of nondairy milk from a grocery store.

Oat milk separates fairly quickly. If you like, you can mix it back up in the blender. Oat milk lasts 3 to 4 days in the fridge.

Once you've made plain unsweetened oat milk, you can create flavors using your favorite sweeteners. Then you can move on to creamers! These are made the same way, just with a higher oat to water ratio. Before you know it, you'll be drinking Oat-chata and London Fog Hot Tea in the day, then having a nightcap of your own Vegan Cream Liqueur. Cheers!

PLAIN UNSWEETENED OAT MILK

SOY-FREE, GLUTEN-FREE, OIL-FREE

Oat milk is so easy to make. It's rich and creamy, plus it's much cheaper than buying some at the store. Steel-cut oats make a thick and creamy milk, but you can add enough water to make it right for you.

MAKES 4 CUPS (946 ML)

4 cups (946 ml) water
1 cup (80 g) steel-cut oats or rolled oats
sweetener of choice to taste, optional

Add the water and oats to your blender and soak. If you are using steel-cut oats, soak for at least 30 minutes; if you are using rolled oats, soak for 10 minutes. Then blend for about 1 to 2 minutes until smooth. Pour the oat mixture through a fine mesh strainer into a pitcher or a bowl with a spout.

You will need to scrape the bottom of the strainer with a spoon when it gets backed up.

Remove the sediment from the strainer, rinse the blender and then strain one more time.

Now you have plain unsweetened oat milk! You can strain back into the blender.

PER SERVING WITH NO PULP REMOVED: Calories 140, protein 6.0 g, total fat 2.5 g, carbohydrates 27.0 g, sodium 0 mg, fiber 4.0 g

{ This milk will keep for about 3 to 4 days in the refrigerator. It will separate, but you can mix it into the blender to get it back together. }

FLAVORED OAT MILK

SOY-FREE, GLUTEN-FREE, OIL-FREE

This recipe starts with a full batch of Plain Unsweetened Oat Milk from page 170. You can use it to make your favorite flavors and create some new ones that you never dreamed possible.

MAKES 4 TO 5 CUPS (946 TO 1183 ML)

OAT MILK BASE

1 batch oat milk (page 170)

FLAVORS TO BLEND IN

VANILLA: 1 teaspoon vanilla extract

CARDAMOM VANILLA: ½ teaspoon cardamom + 1 teaspoon vanilla extract

CHOCOLATE: 2 tablespoons (30 g) cocoa powder

MEXICAN CHOCOLATE: 2 tablespoons (30 g) cocoa powder + ½ teaspoon cinnamon

STRAWBERRY: 1½ cups (225 g) fresh strawberries (strain to remove seeds, and make it a chocolate-covered strawberry by adding 2 tablespoons [30 g] of cocoa powder)

MAPLE: 1 tablespoon (15 ml) maple syrup (or 1 teaspoon maple extract)

PUMPKIN SPICE: ¼ cup (15 g) pumpkin purée + ¾ teaspoon cinnamon + ⅛ teaspoon allspice + pinch nutmeg + pinch cloves

BANANA VANILLA: 1 ripe banana + 1 teaspoon vanilla extract

Mix your chosen flavor option(s) into your plain oat milk and, if you'd like, add your favorite sweetener. The spices and mix-ins may sink to the bottom, so be sure to mix well if you are drinking it a day or two after it's made.

{ This milk will keep for about 3 to 4 days in the refrigerator. It will separate, but you can use your blender to get it back together. }

OAT–CHATA

GLUTEN–FREE, SOY–FREE, OIL–FREE

Horchata is a traditional Mexican beverage made with homemade rice milk, cinnamon and sweeteners. I've taken liberties with it here by adding in oats and almonds. It's amazing served over ice and is the perfect drink for a hot summer day. I have to admit that I went through my first batch in a day—it is just that good. Consider yourself warned. Maybe go ahead and make a double batch.

MAKES 4 CUPS (946 ML)

4 cups (946 ml) water, divided

½ cup (40 g) steel-cut oats

¼ cup (27 g) skinned almonds, whole or slivered

¼ cup (46 g) long grain brown rice

2 whole cinnamon sticks

1 tablespoon (15 ml) agave nectar

1 teaspoon vanilla

⅜ teaspoon stevia

Put 2 cups (473 ml) of the water in a 4-cup (946-ml) sealable glass container along with the oats, almonds, rice and cinnamon. Soak overnight or between 8 to 24 hours.

Once the soaking time is up, remove the cinnamon sticks and pour the mixture into a blender. Blend for 1 to 2 minutes or until most of the particles have broken down.

Strain through a small mesh strainer into a bowl with a pour spout. Rinse the blender and strainer. Strain the mixture a second time into the blender. Add the other 2 cups (473 ml) of the water, agave, vanilla and stevia and blend well.

Store leftovers in the fridge. Serve over ice.

PER CUP WITH NO PULP REMOVED: Calories 185.5, protein 6.0 g, total fat 5.3 g, carbohydrates 29.4 g, sodium 0.1 mg, fiber 3.8 g

- I used my favorite sweetener combination and encourage you to do the same. Just blend the milk with a touch of your sweetener, then taste and add more if necessary.

- For zero waste in this recipe, save the pulp you strain out of this milk and cook it with about 1 to 2 cups (235 to 475 ml) of water over medium heat until the rice particles become soft. I like to eat it as a breakfast with a little sweetener.

VEGAN CREAM LIQUEUR

This is a little like Bailey's and has caramel undertones from the dates. This was inspired by a Scottish drink called Altholl Brose that's actually made with oats but isn't vegan. Try adding this to coffee, pouring over vegan ice cream or drinking on ice.

Please note that not all whiskeys are gluten-free. Make sure to research before buying, since formulas are always changing.

MAKES 2½ CUPS (591 ML)

1 cup (92 g) rolled oats

2 cups (480 ml) water

¼ to ½ cup (60 to 120 ml) whiskey or bourbon, to taste (*Jameson Whiskey is gluten-free)

¼ cup (60 ml) agave nectar

1 teaspoon vanilla extract

4 to 6 dates

Soak the oats in water in blender for 15 minutes. Blend and strain into a bowl with a pour spout. You may need to speed this up once the strainer gets backed up with pulp by scraping a spatula along the bottom of the strainer. Rinse the strainer and blender, then strain back into the blender.

Add the whiskey, agave and vanilla and blend well. Then add in the dates and blend well until the dates have mostly "dissolved" into the mix. (If you don't have a powerful blender, you can soak the dates overnight to soften them up a bit.)

Strain one more time to remove any tiny date bits. Store in the fridge for up to 4 days. You can make smaller batches if you think you won't use it up within that time.

The liqueur will thicken in the fridge, but you can always add extra oat milk or water to thin it. It may also separate some. If it does, just blend again.

PER ¼ CUP (60 ML) SERVING WITH NO PULP REMOVED: Calories 95.4, protein 1.1 g, total fat 0.6 g, carbohydrates 15.0 g, sodium 0.0 mg, fiber 1.1 g

CHOCOLATE MINT CREAMER

GLUTEN-FREE, SOY-FREE, OIL-FREE

This is the perfect winter coffee creamer, but you can put it in your iced coffee in the summer too. The best part of making it yourself is you don't have to be at the mercy of seasonal products at the store.

MAKES ABOUT 1½ CUPS (355 ML)

½ cup (40 g) steel-cut oats (or oat groats soaked overnight and drained)

1½ cups (360 ml) water

2 to 3 tablespoons (14 to 21 g) cocoa powder, to taste

½ teaspoon peppermint extract

½ teaspoon stevia or sweetener of choice, to taste

Put the oats and water in your blender. Let the oats soak for 30 minutes, then blend well and strain out the oat pieces by pouring the creamer through a fine mesh strainer into a small bowl.

Rinse the blender and strain again into the blender. Add the cocoa powder and peppermint extract, then blend well.

Store in the fridge for up to 3 to 5 days.

PER ¼ CUP (60 ML) SERVING WITH NO PULP REMOVED: Calories 91.2, protein 4.0 g, total fat 1.9 g, carbohydrates 16.5 g, sodium 0.6 mg, fiber 3.4 g

{ Leave out the mint extract to make a plain chocolate creamer, or substitute it with orange extract for one of my favorite flavor combinations. }

COCONUT OAT VANILLA NUT CREAMER

GLUTEN-FREE, SOY-FREE, OIL-FREE

This creamer gives you the same fun flavor without all the fillers. You can play with the extracts you use to change flavors.

MAKES 1 CUP (237 ML)

¼ cup (24 g) rolled oats

¼ cup (24 g) finely shredded coconut

1 cup (237 ml) water

1 tablespoon (15 ml) agave nectar (or sweetener of choice, to taste)

1 teaspoon vanilla extract

¼ to ½ teaspoon almond extract, to taste

Break the oats and coconut into tiny pieces with your blender. Add the water and let soak for 10 minutes.

Blend again for about 3 minutes or until smooth, then run the creamer through a fine mesh strainer over a small bowl to strain out the oat pieces.

Put the liquid, sweetener and extracts back in the blender and blend until the sweetener is incorporated and dissolved.

PER ¼ CUP (60 ML) SERVING WITH NO PULP REMOVED: Calories 83.8, protein 1.1 g, total fat 5.4 g, carbohydrates 9.4 g, sodium 2.5 mg, fiber 1.5 g

- There will be about 1 cup (200 g) of pulp left over. Save this for the dog cookie recipe on page 188.

- You can use steel-cut oats in place of rolled; just increase the soaking time to 30 minutes.

LONDON FOG HOT TEA

GLUTEN-FREE, SOY-FREE, OIL-FREE

London Fog is traditionally a tea made with Earl Grey, vanilla syrup and rich steamed milk. Oat creamer is already thick and rich, so adding in pure vanilla and your favorite sweetener makes this the healthier option, while still feeling decadent. You'll never be able to get this at that large chain store!

MAKES 2 CUPS (473 ML)

½ cup (48 g) rolled oats

1 cup (237 ml) water

1 to 2 tablespoons (15 to 30 ml) agave nectar (or sweetener of choice, to taste)

1 teaspoon vanilla extract or seeds scraped from ½ vanilla bean pod

1 cup (235 ml) brewed double-strength Earl Grey Tea (Use twice as much tea and brew for 4 minutes if using black tea, 2 to 3 if using green tea or 7 to 8 for rooibos)

Let the oats and water sit in your blender for 10 minutes to let the oats soften. Blend until the mixture is as smooth as possible. To strain out the oat pieces, put a fine mesh strainer over a small bowl and pour the mixture through it.

Put the oat cream you just made, sweetener and extracts back in the blender and blend until the sweetener is incorporated and dissolved. If you don't like it this thick, you can always add another ¼ cup (60 ml) of water and blend again.

You can use this in your tea at room temperature, but if you have a high-speed blender, you can blend it on a high speed to heat up the vanilla oat milk. Pour into a hot mug of freshly brewed Earl Grey Tea and enjoy!

Note: If you heat the creamer in the microwave or on the stove, it will thicken.

PER CUP WITH NO PULP REMOVED: Calories 111, protein 2.5 g, total fat 1.5 g, carbohydrates 21.8 g, sodium 0.2 mg, fiber 2.0 g

{ Ditch the tea and make a vanilla latte with coffee instead! If you don't use all the flavored oat milk, you can keep it in the fridge for 3 to 4 days. I like mine milky, so I use it all! }

HOT CHOCOLATE MIX

Here's an allergy-free hot chocolate mix that is portable, too! You can customize it with your favorite spices like cinnamon or cardamom. It's also perfect to keep at the office for a guilt-free afternoon treat!

MAKES 8 SERVINGS

½ cup (48 g) rolled oats

½ cup (43 g) cocoa powder

1 tablespoon (12 g) coconut sugar

1 teaspoon stevia powder or ½ cup (100 g) brown or coconut sugar

pinch of salt

Blend all of the ingredients together to a fine powder. Store in an airtight container.

To use: Add 2 tablespoons (30 g) of mix to 1 cup (237 ml) hot water or nondairy milk.

PER 2 TABLESPOON (30 G) SERVING: Calories 36.7, protein 1.7 g, total fat 1.1 g, carbohydrates 7.8 g, sodium 4.5 mg, fiber 2.3 g

{ Hate thin cocoa? After you mix the powder into your hot water or milk, pop your mug into the microwave for 30 seconds. It will thicken the oats just enough for you to feel like you are drinking a hot chocolate from a café! }

CHAPTER NINE

BEYOND THE DINING ROOM: OTHER USES FOR OATS

Just when you thought oats had reached their limit, here are a few uses that you may not have considered.

If you look at some of your expensive bath salts and scrubs, you may be surprised to find oats in the ingredient list. They are sometimes referred to as colloidal oatmeal. The great news is you don't need to go to a chemistry class to make it; all you need is a strong blender or a spice or coffee grinder.

Finely ground oats added to a bath are soothing to dry or sunburned skin and can even alleviate itching, which makes it great to have on hand in the winter. You can use it as is or make the Soothing Lavender Oat Bath Soak to leave you (and your bathroom) smelling beautiful!

I like to use the Oatmeal Cookie Scrub on my dry hands, but it's delightful to use on your whole body in the shower. The best part is that you probably already have the ingredients you need to make the scrub right in your kitchen!

Some of the better doggie cookies have oats as a main ingredient. I have a gluten-free cookie recipe, as well as recipes featuring peppermint for better breath and culinary grade lavender and chamomile for calming your energetic pup.

You will not believe how cheap these are to make at home. In fact, if you start making oat milk on a weekly basis, you'll find yourself with a surplus of oat pulp. Instead of just throwing it away, use it in a recipe like the Calm Pup Cookies. You could replace some of the banana with it in the other doggie cookies as well.

I couldn't leave the kitties out, so there's also a recipe that includes catnip. After all, your cats need a little fun and relaxation, too!

SOOTHING LAVENDER OAT BATH SOAK

Itchy skin is no fun, but relaxing in a warm and moisturizing bath of Lavender Oat Bath Soak certainly is. Just chalk up another point for oats!

MAKES 2½ CUPS (592 G)

2 cups (184 g) rolled oats

½ cup (110 g) baking soda

2 tablespoons (28 g) lavender buds

2 tablespoons (30 ml) olive oil

2 tablespoons (10 ml) rosewater

Grind the oats, baking soda and lavender into a fine powder using a blender or spice grinder. Add in the olive oil and rosewater. Store in an airtight jar and use ¼ to ½ cup (60 to 120 ml) per bath.

{ Make variations by using other herbs and extracts. }

OATMEAL COOKIE SCRUB

This scrub is gentle and moisturizing, and it uses ingredients that you have on hand. It can also be tucked in a mason jar with a ribbon for a quick and easy present.

MAKES 2 CUPS (160 G)

1 cup (92 g) rolled oats
¾ cup (165 g) brown sugar
¼ cup (240 ml) olive oil
1 tablespoon (15 ml) vanilla extract
1½ teaspoons (4 g) ground cinnamon

Grind the oats into a fine powder using a blender or spice grinder. Mix all the ingredients in a bowl using a fork or your hands to distribute the moisture evenly. Store in an airtight jar.

CALM PUP COOKIES

SOY-FREE, OIL-FREE, GLUTEN-FREE OPTION*

Lavender and chamomile can be a stressed doggie's best friend. Instead of spending a fortune on tinctures, make some of these cookies to relieve a little of your own stress. My dogs love these. They really help my high-strung pup relax.

MAKES ABOUT 3 DOZEN MEDIUM BONE-SHAPED COOKIES

½ cup leftover oat pulp (from making oat milk or creamer—page 170)

1 tablespoon (7 g) ground flaxseed

2 small bananas

1 tablespoon (4 g) crushed dried chamomile flowers

1 tablespoon (14 g) culinary lavender

1½ cups (140 g) rolled oats

1¼ to 1½ cups (160 to 195 g) whole wheat flour (*use gluten-free baking mix)

Preheat the oven to 350°F (177°C). Oil 2 cookie sheets or cover with parchment paper.

In a mixer or a large bowl, mash the pulp, flaxseed and bananas until the mixture is relatively smooth. Add in the herbs and oats, and then incorporate the whole wheat flour a ½ cup (65 g) at a time. You may have to knead in the last bit of flour with your hands.

Flour a large cutting board and roll out the dough. Take care to keep the board floured as you go along so that it's easy to get the cookies off. Roll the dough to about ¼-inch/0.6-cm thick and use either your favorite cookie cutter or a pizza cutter to cut out fun shapes.

Move the cookies to the cookie sheets as you go along. Gather any remaining dough, roll out, cut more cookies and repeat until all the dough is used.

Alternatively, if you don't have the time or energy to roll out the dough and make cute cookies, just press the batter evenly on the cookie sheet with your hands. Take a dough scraper or knife and score the dough.

Bake for 40 minutes. You can leave them like this and have softer cookies with a crisp bottom, or you can break the pieces off, turn them upside down and spread onto 2 large cookie sheets and bake for an additional 10 to 15 minutes.

GLUTEN-FREE SWEET POTATO BANANA DOGGIE BISCUITS

SOY-FREE, GLUTEN-FREE

Dogs are developing allergies as quickly as people are these days. Both of our dogs have food allergies, so I have a recipe for you to try if yours do as well. These are full of banana, sweet potato, coconut oil and parsley—all things that make a good doggie feel even better.

MAKES ABOUT 72 1-TABLESPOON (30-G) SIZED COOKIES

2 very ripe bananas

¾ cup (135 g) sweet potato purée (can use pumpkin instead)

⅓ cup (69 ml) coconut oil

2 tablespoons (3 g) parsley (fresh or dried)

2 cups (240 g) buckwheat flour

1 cup (92 g) rolled oats

1 teaspoon baking soda

½ teaspoon cinnamon

1 cup (158 g) brown rice flour

Preheat oven to 350°F (177°C). Spread 2 cookie sheets with parchment paper or spray them with oil.

Combine the bananas, sweet potato purée, coconut oil and parsley in a mixer until smooth and creamy. Add in the buckwheat flour, mix, then add the oats, baking soda and cinnamon.

Mix some more, then add the brown rice flour ½ cup (75 g) at a time.

The dough will not be stiff enough to roll out, so use a tablespoon cookie scoop and place dollops about 1 inch (2.5 cm) apart. Smash them flat with the palm of your hand or the back of a wooden spoon.

Bake for 10 minutes. When you take them out of the oven, flip them on the cookie sheet and let cool. This will cook the tops a little more and increase their shelf-life.

Repeat until all the cookies are baked. Store in an airtight container. If you don't want that many cookies all at once, you can pack up some of the dough in wax paper and freeze it. When you are ready, cut thin slices of the dough and bake for a quick good-dog treat.

PEPPERMINT PUPPY COOKIES

SOY-FREE

I also call these Quiet Cookies because I used them to teach my pups to stop barking. Now, when I ask if they want a Quiet Cookie, my dogs come to me silently and sit patiently for their tasty treat. Their minty-fresh breath is just an added bonus!

MAKES ABOUT 6 CUPS (360 G) COOKIES OR COOKIE PIECES

1 cup (208 g) coconut oil

¼ cup (112 g) ground flaxseed mixed with ½ cup (120 ml) warm water

2 ripe bananas, broken into small pieces

½ cup (127 g) unsweetened applesauce

2 teaspoons (10 ml) peppermint extract

3 cups (375 g) white whole wheat flour

2 cups (160 g) rolled oats

1 teaspoon salt

Oil a large cookie sheet and preheat the oven to 350°F (177°C).

Cream the coconut oil, flaxseed mixture, bananas, applesauce and peppermint together in a mixer (or mash together using a pastry cutter) until the banana is mashed well and the coconut oil is thoroughly incorporated.

Add the salt, 2 cups (200 g) of the white wheat flour and 1 cup (80 g) of the rolled oats. Mix well, then add the oats and remaining flour.

Press the batter evenly on the cookie sheet, spreading it into each corner. Take a dough scraper or knife and score the dough.

Bake for 40 minutes. You can leave them like this and have softer cookies with a crisp bottom, or you can break the pieces off, turn them upside down and spread onto 2 large cookie sheets, baking for an additional 10 to 15 minutes.

CATNIP KITTY TREATS

GLUTEN-FREE, SOY-FREE, OIL-FREE

If you have a mixed-species household like I do, you better be bringing the cats a treat if the dogs are snacking. Irma, my older cat, has a special evil look if there's no cookie for her!

MAKES 2 TO 2½ CUPS (340 TO 426 G) OF TINY TREATS

2½ cups (232 g) rolled oats

2 tablespoons (12 g) nutritional yeast

¼ cup (114 g) dried and crushed catnip

⅔ cup (150 g) nondairy yogurt

Preheat the oven to 350°F (177°C) and spray a small cookie sheet with oil.

Blend the oats, yeast and catnip until the oats are ground as fine as flour. Pour into a mixing bowl and stir in the yogurt to create the dough.

Press the dough out about ⅛ to ¼-inch (0.3 to 0.6-cm) thin on the cookie sheet and score the dough so it's easier to break up into tiny treats when finished baking.

Bake for 20 minutes. You can stop here if you want chewy treats; just make sure to store them in the fridge. If you do not, the moisture will make them go bad faster at room temperature.

If you want crunchy treats, bake for the original 20 minutes and then let cool until comfortable to the touch. Then break apart into individual treats and bake for an additional 5 to 10 minutes. They should be fairly hard—like biscotti.

 No yogurt? You can use nondairy milk, broth or even water in its place.

INGREDIENT RESOURCES

I always feel lucky living in the age of the Internet because no matter where you live, you can get almost anything delivered right to your door. Various versions of oat, spices, extracts and oils are just a few clicks away on the web!

OATS

If you are having trouble locating oats in your local grocery, you can order online from one of these companies.

• Bob's Red Mill
• Coach's Oats
• Country Choice

SPICES

If you have a nearby co-op or shop that sells spices in bulk, then that should be your first stop. You can get tiny amounts this way so you aren't stuck with something you may end up not liking.

Indian groceries are a perfect and inexpensive source for spices. Hispanic groceries are a playground of fresh and dried chilies. You can toast the whole dried chilies in the oven until crumbly, but not burnt, and grind them in a spice grinder for the freshest chili powder you will ever taste!

These are the brand you'll usually find locally in bulk bins, but you can also order online:

• My Spice Sage
• Savory Spice Shop
• Penzeys
• Frontier

OILS AND EXTRACTS

My favorite source for pure citrus oils and other extracts is Boyajian. I actually met the founder at Longhouse, a conference for food writers. He was as delightful as his oils. You can get them online at Amazon.com and in some wholesale stores, like Costco. You can get more details on them and their other products at boyajianinc.com.

ACKNOWLEDGMENTS

This is my first book with Page Street Publishing, and I love working with Will Keister. I am glad to have Lisa and Sally Ekus by (and on) my side and appreciate their great advice as agents and as friends.

My fearless testers are wonderful people and amazing cooks, and I can't possibly thank them enough: Rochelle Arvizo, Kirsten Barry, Debbie Blicher, Monika Soria Caruso, Julie Cross, Vicki Brett-Gach, Jessica Ledford, Ann Oliverio, Anna Pelzer, Dianne Weinz and Ruth Zaugg.

Many thanks to Marissa Giambelluca, Ashley Yee and Debbie Blicher for doing an excellent editing job. I am thrilled with Meg Baskis's wonderful layout for this book. The wonderful photography is the work of photographer Kate Lewis, www.kk-lewis.com.

I can't possibly thank Cheryl Purser enough, although she did score another trip to Disney. This time it was even to Disneyland! Much appreciation to my friends for not disowning me during my time as a hermit. I promise to have many dinner parties to make up for it!

ABOUT THE AUTHOR

Kathy Hester is the author of *Vegan Slow Cooking for Two or Just You*, *The Great Vegan Bean Book* and the best-selling *The Vegan Slow Cooker*. She loves to show people how easy it is to cook healthy at home.

She posts easy recipes on her blog, healthyslowcooking.com, writes a weekly vegan column for Key Ingredient (www.keyingredient.com) and writes for various blogs, sites and publications.

She lives in Durham, North Carolina, with a grown-up picky eater, 2 quirky dogs and 2 cats—who still would rather not live together—in her 1970s modernist dreamhouse.

INDEX